ALL THINGS WORK TOGETHER

Nothing is off Limits

BY

PORCHIA CARTER

All Things Work Together

ISBN: 9798694151375

Editing by Ashley Fleming
Cover Design by The Carter's Touch
Photography by The Carter's Touch
Book Writing Coach: Darlyshia Menzie, Fervent Servant Book Coaching Services, www.ferventservant.life

Bulk Ordering Information: Quantity sales. Special discounts are available on quantity purchases by groups, churches, ministry associations, and others. For details to reach out and contact the author at contact@porchiacarter.com.

Printed in the United States of America.

This book describes occurrences in the life of Porchia Carter according to the author's memory and perspective. All of the stories are her truths. However, some names and identifying details have been changed to keep the privacy of those involved.

Scripture Reference

Romans 8:28 (NKJV)

"And we know that all things work together for good to those who love God, to those who are the called according to His Purpose."

Dedication

I dedicate this book to my wonderful siblings. It is my prayer that each of us grasp the understanding of the promise in this scripture and take on life knowing that God has our backs always. May each of you flourish in your callings with everything God has placed inside of you. The special places you all have in my heart will never be tainted. I love you all so much from the very bottom of my heart.

Kris Catchings
Deborah "Pooh Pooh" Catchings
Shonte' Ragland
Titus "Danny" Carter, Jr.
Israel Carter
Jireh Carter
Tiyonna Carter
Aniah Carter
Halina Carter
Soter Carter
Kyran Carter

Thank Yous

THANK YOU JESUS!!!!! This has been a journey! Nevertheless, any journey with you is forever and always worth taking. Thank you for always being there for me and never leaving me or forsaking me like you said in your word. Thank you for calling me and allowing me to complete this book. Thank you for making me an Author! It's almost unreal to me. Thank you that your will for my life is far greater than what I could have ever planned out or imagined. Thank you for blessing me with a transparent heart to cultivate a space of healing for myself and others. I love you God so much, and I will continue this saying "yes" thing until you call me up out of here!

Thank you to my parents for giving me life and blessing me with the opportunity to be introduced to Jesus at an early age. That was the most important gift from a mother to a daughter for me. Thank you Mama. The cultivating of that gift was the best decision any father could have made. Thank you Daddy. You guys have been at the deepest place of love in my heart since I was born, and you will remain there forever. I love you both to unexplainable measures.

Thank you so much to all of my friends and family who have been there for me and supported me through every stage of life!

Thank you all for always rooting for me. Thank you all for praying for me. I love you all so much.

Special thanks to my aunty/second-mama Aunty Kesha Robinson, my best friend/sister Stephanie Durr, my prayer-partner/sister Olamide K. Giwa, and my aunty/spiritual counselor Aunty Tara Carter. I love y'all.

Contents

Introduction

Now You Know

If you ever found yourself in a situation that was a little shaky or didn't quite make sense, then you probably didn't *know* at all what the outcome would be like for you. We have all been there in places in our lives where we asked the question, why me? Why is this happening to me? Why isn't this working out for me? Why was I born in this type of predicament and with these types of people? How could this ever work out in my favor? Or what is the painful situation trying to teach me? If you're anything like me, then these questions become the loudest thoughts in your head when you're going through a tough time in life. And if that be the case, then keep on reading, because this book is for you!

Romans 8:28 (NKJV) says, *"And we know that all things work together for good to those who love God, to those who are the called according to His Purpose."* Let's take a further look into what this actually means. The first part of the scripture starts out by stating that *"we know."* There are so many times in life that we ignore what *we know* and act out of our temporary frustrations. This has happened to me often. I know I'm only in my 20s, but I can definitely tell you that when unplanned things have happened in my life, I have still chosen to react out of emotions like I never even heard of Him before, even though I've known about God the majority of my lifespan. The thing is, we as people tend to ignore everything that *we know* when the walls come crashing down on us because we let our emotions and feelings take over. What you feel should never overpower what you *know*. I write this book with hope that whoever reads it can grasp a knowing of the promise in this scripture for their own lives. When you really *know* something, no one can ever take that away from you.

The next part of the scripture tells us *what* we know. It says, *"All things work together for good."* That one phrase alone should be enough for you to continue worshipping God every time something crazy happens in your life. The crazier the situation is, the greater your reward for trusting God through it. Whether the situation is good or bad, it is all meant to *work for your good*. There is nothing that God allows in your life that doesn't have the capability to *work* out in your favor. God only permits things to happen to you that He intends to use in the process of building your character. He is intentional about all of your trials, especially the ones that hurt you the most. You can rest in knowing that God knew about it before it happened. He already knew how you would feel about it. He also already knew how you would break through it. He just wants you to trust Him while He is creating the masterpiece of who you are. It takes every single detail, whether it be a test, trial, happiness, hurt, joy, pain, suffering, or even trauma to be pieced *together* in order to form a masterpiece. Once you begin to see your life how God sees it, you will praise Him in those times when the tough things happen, and you will rest in knowing that He is still working. But not only is He working, once He's done, everything will be all *good*.

We will visit the last part of this scripture in the conclusion. Until we get there, here's what you can expect as you continue reading: This book is filled with various stories in my life where I didn't *know* how I was going to get through some type of difficult situation, traumatic experience, or painful results of some detrimental decisions I had made. Some of these experiences have been too painful to think about or too embarrassing to speak out loud. I didn't quite grasp the concept of knowing that God can use even the dirtiest of things to work for my good until this book. I mean I got down and low to some points of questioning my very existence. The transparency you will read from this point on was extremely hard for me to share, but it has created a space of healing for me. At the end of each chapter I explain how each topic *worked for my good.* And *now I Know* the truth of this promise and will be able to fight the whirlwind of confusion when other things come up.

My prayer is that you can walk away from this book reviewing your own life stories and receive healing in every area of your life as well. May you now *know* what "this thing" you're dealing with was meant for, what it was supposed to teach you, or how God used it to protect you from something else. He can pull you out of anything and turn absolutely anything around to *work for your good.* Nothing is off limits. If you leave out of a circumstance or look back at a circumstance only to gain perspective, then that thing has worked! *Now you know, that it is good.*

Chapter One

Growing Pains Work

I grew up in a neighborhood on the eastside of Detroit. We lived on a street called Houston Whittier, between the main streets Chalmers and Gratiot. We were deeply afflicted by poverty. I spent the majority of my childhood with my mama and my siblings born from her. My mama has four children. The pack included my brother Kris, who is 10 years older than I am, my sister Deborah "Pooh Pooh," who is 2 years my senior, myself, and my little sister Shonte', who is only 1 year younger than I am. Our lives consisted of attending school, playing outside with our neighbors, and going to church. We were in church literally every day of the week whenever we weren't at school. We had Sunday services all day long. Monday school; Tuesday prayer at church; Wednesday Bible Study; Thursday school; Friday sometimes worship nights or shut-ins; Saturday whatever fun day event they would create for us to be there; then Sunday, church all day again. It was almost as if my mama was addicted to church. As children, we really didn't understand, nor did we think it was a bad thing, we just wanted to be "normal," and spending our lives at church didn't seem that normal for me.

Our neighborhood friends had regular lives. They were able to go to school with us, and then play outside all day long without even having to look at a church building until Sunday. Pooh Pooh, Shonte' and I never really complained about being in church all the time, we just wanted more time with friends during the day. Kris on the other hand, was not at all into being at church that frequently, so when he turned 16, he stopped going to church altogether. Once he stopped going, I guess my mama felt like she could leave us at home with him while she attended her every night church festivities. That lasted for a while until we started begging to go with her again, because our brother would fight us, treating us like we were his life-sized wrestling toys whenever she was gone. We were only little girls, and with him being way older and stronger than we were it was unbearable, so we preferred to be at church.

We lived in a very fragmented home. The eastside of Detroit wasn't always as ruthless and deserted as it is now, so to have a house in the area we were living in at the time was cool. We had a pretty nice sized 3-bedroom house with a basement and attic to play in. But over time, our house turned into an awful story. We used to have friends and family over frequently, and then once our house was fully run down, people weren't over as much anymore. My aunty did hair out of the house for a while, but that stopped eventually too. Our home wasn't always the way I'm about to explain, but for as much as I could remember, when it got bad, it was really bad. The house was filthy and messy. The bottom of our feet would be black from just a day of walking around it without shoes. It was unwholesome and made mice feel welcomed to invade our home, which is the reason I'm scared of ALL rodents to this very day. They would bite my fingers in my sleep, there were so many of them. And the smell after leaving mouse traps everywhere was enough to make you puke! There were roaches, as you could imagine, and I can't even tell you how many spiders and webs were in the basement. It felt like a haunted house to say the least. We had burned kitchen floors with writings on just about every wall on the house. Yes, we the children were probably to blame for how messy our house was, but we were rarely instructed to clean it up. Plus, we really didn't know how.

Not only did we live in a mess, but we were poor which made the situation worse. I remember times when we were so low on food that Vienna sausages or spam were all we had to eat for dinner. Mayo sandwiches and hot dogs were also a go to. Nothing wrong with that, but once the food stamps ran out, we could feel it. We didn't have money for multiple expensive school uniform shirts, so we often recycled the ones we had. We seemed to always have our stuff together for holidays though. Easter and Christmas were our favorite holidays. Our hair would be pressed and curled (ears burnt from the pressing), and my sisters and I had the best of the best dresses for those occasions. Food was always plentiful, and my mama's cake baking was amazing! Growing up there wasn't all bad. We had a lot of great times and enjoyed every season we had in that house. However, I'm not sure if the cause of our environment was due to work or church and school busyness, but I do know it wasn't safe.

We received a rude awakening about our living condition when Child Protective Services (CPS) showed up to our house for a random inspection. I was 9 years old, and the very thought of being taken away from my mother was enough to equate to death. My sisters and I cried and cried and cried when we were told what was happening to us. We were kids and didn't understand the magnitude of our living condition. We knew that we couldn't have company or sleepovers like our friends at church were having, but we just thought it was due to our room not being cleaned. We were so scared that we'd be taken away and separated that we didn't have time to process it all. This was the very first time I ever prayed in my life. I remember being in my mama's car listening to every song on the *Incredible* album by Mary Mary really closely for them to explain how I could pray my way out of this situation. It worked. I don't remember the prayer, but I know I asked God to please not take me away from my mommy and sisters.

The social worker who came to our home gave us a week to get our house in order, or we were out of there. So, we cleaned our house for a week from top to bottom. We scrubbed walls, mopped floors, cleaned sinks, and did things that we never had to do before then. Family members came over to help as well. Next thing I knew, we had new furniture in our rooms and our house was the most presentable it had ever been in roughly two whole years. We were spared, and allowed to stay with our mama, but that idea of child neglect that had formed in the process was still there.

Towards the end of my fourth grade year of school, my Aunty Kesha came to pick us up from my mama's house so we could stay with her for a while. Now Aunty Kesha has a big heart for children. She is intentional about building personal relationships with children who need it the most so that they can have someone to turn to in hard times. Not only that, she is fun and outgoing, and loved taking us to movies, carnivals, the state fair, and every fun activity her church came up with. While we were staying with her, she noticed that we had been going to school with dirty clothes on, so she took our tan school shirts and made them white again. We went to Detroit Edison Public School Academy where we had to wear red, black and white plaid colored skirts with a tie to match. The only color shirt we could wear with our uniform was white, and since we didn't have a plethora of those, getting them dirty wasn't hard. She took us to school and made sure we were picked up and brought to the beauty shop after. She is a hair stylist, so she did our hair every day until she found someone to braid our hair up throughout the summer.

We spent that entire summer with Aunty Kesha in her one-bedroom apartment. This was really the best time of my elementary life. Our cousin Diamond spent the summer with us there as well. She would dance with me to every music video we were able to watch. This was like an escape for my sisters and me because my mama didn't play that. We weren't allowed to listen to "worldly music" in her house, and we couldn't even watch *106 & Park*. But at Aunty Kesha's house, we watched and listened to it all. This was the time in my life where my dream was to be a background dancer for Ciara. Her videos were my favorite and I just had to learn every dance routine to every video that summer. I had already grown a love for dance from dancing in church and joining our elementary school dance team. I just knew after the summer at Aunty Kesha's place, I was going to grow up to be a dancer.

The name of the street we lived on with Aunty Kesha was Chelsea. And boy do we have so many "Chelsea stories." I think once we moved in with Aunty Kesha, everybody on the block knew who we were. Kids around the neighborhood would meet us out front to go across the street and play at the playground. We had tons of outside fun and had our own mini parties in the house with Aunty Kesha after she did hair all day. She taught us how to hip roll and win money at dance contests. The song she made up for it was hilarious and I still joke about it with them to this day. We had a ball taking over the neighborhood and getting to know everyone on the block. But before I knew it, things had happened back at our house that left us homeless and my mama moved into Aunty Kesha's apartment with us.

By the time school came back around, my aunty realized that the one bedroom apartment was too small for all of us to keep living there. We moved into a bigger house. We all lived there together for a short amount of time, before my mama was forced to find somewhere else for us to go. My aunty and Mama got into a fight, then the next thing I knew we were walking miles and miles to some motel Mama found. We had nowhere to go, and we couldn't afford to live in a motel. So, my mama gathered us up, excluding my older brother, and took us to a homeless shelter. I don't really remember where my brother went, but I know he did not go to that shelter with us. At the time, I wish I wasn't going to that shelter with us either.

Life in the shelter was pretty sad for a young girl who never thought she would experience such a thing. Not only that, I cared so much about my mama and sisters that seeing them sad made the pain twice as hard to deal with. I tried to shake it off though. I was on the dance team at school, so I focused all of my energy on dancing. I danced hard at practice and went full out, performing at our basketball games. Dance became my outlet. I went to school depressed for about a month. But when my moping started to alarm my teachers, I got my act together, because I didn't want CPS coming for my mama again.

We lived in that homeless shelter for at least six months straight. I don't really remember the full timeline, but it felt like a year! The majority of my fifth grade life was spent there. Although I was only 10 years old, I was stressed out. I worried every night. Sometimes I would hear my mama or one of my sisters crying in the middle of the night while everyone was asleep, and that would hurt me so deeply. I silently cried sometimes too but didn't want anyone else to see me hurt. It hurt so badly to the point where my hair began to fall out. I went from having hair that was shoulder length long, to barely being able to put it into a ponytail. This happened only within one month. I hadn't noticed until one day on my way to school, the rubber band holding my hair together popped. I had to use my bracelet to try to pull a ponytail together, but it didn't work. I couldn't remember how I managed to get the rubber band on. I was on the city bus and people were staring at me while I tried to work my short hair into a miracle, and all I could do was cry.

We spent Christmas in the shelter that year as well. Due to God's favor on our lives our family was adopted by another family who showered us abundantly with Christmas gifts at some big Christmas event hosted by the city of Detroit every year. We were grateful, because without them, we would have been extremely miserable that Christmas for having no presents outside of our usual "good fellow box." I didn't think those winter months there weren't too bad though, because we were allowed to go outside and play in the snow with other kids who happened to live in the shelter as well. The issue was that we had to catch the city bus to school in that same snow because my mama no longer had a car. With us being young girls and having to wear skirts as school uniforms, it was a very traumatic experience to my legs and feet daily. We had to take a SMART bus and I believe two DDOT buses to drive us to school from the shelter. It was a lot.

The worst part about being there was when I had to spend my eleventh birthday in that shelter. I couldn't even have a cake because bringing any type of outside food into the shelter was forbidden. No candy, no snacks, no nothing. They did feed us breakfast, lunch, and dinner in the cafeteria, so I'm assuming their "no outside food" policy was just so the rooms could stay clean. We started out on a pretty clean floor which was the first floor.

That floor was filled with old women, women with special needs children, and single women without any kids, so it was pretty clean and quiet. But after a few months, they transferred us from the first floor to the third floor.

There wasn't anything good you would ever hear about the third floor. It was for women with children, and that meant all age ranges. To my surprise there were women there who had infants and even newborn babies, so you heard babies crying often throughout the night. Living on that floor was a full tale of its own. I was young, so at this point in my life I just tried to make the best out of living there. I tried making friends, playing around, and having fun the best way I knew how. We didn't have TV there, so our entertainment was other kids, and getting into all kinds of possible trouble in the meantime.

After months of living in the shelter, we finally rented our own place. It was a nice big two-family flat home. We lived in the house on the bottom of the flat, and the house on top was occupied by another family we made friends with at the shelter. During that time, things began to turn around for us. I thought that we would never be homeless again. We had food, we had clothes, and we even kept this new house of ours super clean and put together. We used to skate around the poles in the basement and have little concerts.

My mama bought a TV during that time which was extremely outdated. I mean it was so old it looked like it was from the 60s, and we were currently living in the year 2005. The only thing I enjoyed watching on it was the Pistons playing in the NBA finals. They had won the championship a year prior, so we just knew they were going to win again. We were expecting celebrations, parades, and for the whole city of Detroit to be in an exciting uproar for consecutive wins! When they didn't win, I felt upset. Not because

I had a love for basketball or anything. I was just rooting for our team the same way I was rooting for my life. For the first time in my life, I understood the phrase "good times come and go, but the memories last forever." This would be the tale of my life as I dealt with more homelessness in the future.

How This Worked For Me

"For I know the plans I have for you," declares the Lord, "plans to prosper you and not to harm you, plans to give you hope and a future."

Jeremiah 29:11 (NIV)

Growing up in a broken home and dealing with homelessness can be a lot on any young heart. I believe this circumstance planted seeds of worry in my mind pertaining to stability. This wasn't the last time throughout my life where I found myself in a state of having no home. This has always been an area of my life that became extremely tough to trust God in. However, He showed me that even in the shelter, He had favor on our lives. Although I may have been distraught at first, He kept me. Anything could have happened to us in that shelter, but we were safe. We were fed. We made it to school every single day. We still made friends and had fun to the best of our ability.

When I think back to that particular growing pain, I see how it taught me the essence of appreciation. I can always appreciate whenever I have a place to call my own. I am able to take care of the places I live in with a heart of gratitude. I don't ever take the gift of having a roof over my head for granted. What I went through back then only made me stronger for all of the things I would face in the future. Being able to make it out of there prepared me to make it out of lots of things to follow. It also gave me a heart of compassion for people living without a place to call home. I know that what God creates out of this passion in my heart for the homeless will be good. I believe wonderful initiatives are birthed out of people's past experiences. If the growing pains I experienced were all for the sake of someone else, then it was all good.

Chapter Two

Daddy Issues Work

I have always desired to sport the title "Daddy's Girl." I see little girls with their daddies on social media, in TV and movies, out in public, or even just talking to friends who consider themselves daddy's girls. When I am exposed to those types of father-daughter relationships, it gets hard for me not to wonder what my life would have been like if I grew up that way. I sometimes imagine having my daddy in my home from the time I was born until the time I went to college. I fantasize about how the choices I made would have been different and less painful if my daddy was there for me consistently from birth so that I could have understood the importance of receiving love, protection, provision, encouragement and all the other things girls are supposed to have from a father. Spending the majority of my life's years without him left voids in my heart that I tried to fill with men, sex, and a whole bunch of other destructive things that could have been avoided.

Although my parents had a wedding, they never married. Luckily for me, I was already in my mama's stomach before the outrageous separation. From my perspective, I was the result of a perfect love story that lasted only for a split second before real life struck again. The outcome of that was me growing up not knowing who my real father was until I was around 7 years old. That's the earliest memory I have of meeting him. My daddy and I actually have a good relationship now, but my formative years were spent without him due to distance. The few years I was able to spend with him during my school years were filled with him trying to make me unlearn what I learned growing up with my mama so that I could be something he saw for me. I didn't realize it then, but the damage of growing up in a single parent home was already done. And the work he tried to do in such a short time would be to no avail given the circumstances of this attempt.

In all the years of my Detroit life, there was no father in our home, so all the love we received and knew how to receive came from our mother. I do vaguely remember when I was about four or five years of age when my stepdad, the father of my older and younger sister, visited quite often. That time was short though, because soon after we were headed to Canada every weekend to visit him and his new wife. On some weekends, he and our mama would take us to Belle Isle to feed the deer and the ducks that took over where the Belle Isle Zoo used to be.

For a while I thought that he was my dad, until my younger sister and I got into a fight one day, and she told me that I needed to leave her daddy alone because it was her daddy and not mine. I told my stepdad what she said, and he looked me in my eyes, and he asked me, "Who have you always known to be your daddy?" I said, "You." He said, "Okay then, and I will always be there for you." Although I was still confused, I said okay and didn't think anything of it anymore. However, shortly after that we stopped going to Canada on the weekends to visit him. It would be years before we reconnected with him again.

Those feelings of confusion and abandonment didn't creep back again until I met my real daddy a couple years later when I was about 7 years of age. After that, I felt like the outcast. I never wanted to feel separated from my sisters. My daddy had family who attended our church. Over the years I had been introduced to cousins, aunties and even my grandma before I remember meeting my daddy. After realizing I had a different extended family, I didn't mind when my paternal family would pick me up from church or home without the company of my sisters. Aside from my brother, I was the middle child in the group of girls, so I had no idea I'd be singled out, until I was.

In the fall when I was about 8 years of age and in third grade, my daddy came from where he lived in Atlanta to take me home with him. He had a wife and four children younger than me. His other son Danny, who is 8 years older than I am, had come from Detroit to stay with him too. Meeting my 5 new siblings was confusing and exciting all at once for me. At this point, I now had a total of 8 siblings including the 3 I had lived with back in Detroit. But in the process of trying to adjust to a new big family, I again began to feel like an outcast.

I honestly can't recall any quality father-daughter time during those nine or so months of living there. I still didn't quite get a grasp of who he was or what he was supposed to mean to my life. He had so many other children to tend to at the time, while also being a truck driver, so his absence was still at the forefront of my heart. I didn't stay there long that time. When my third grade year ended, Danny's mom came to get both of us one night to take us back to Detroit. I was soon to be reunited with my mama and siblings whom I loved and missed dearly.

Returning home to Detroit after a school year spent with my family in the South felt amazing. I was not only reunited with my mama and siblings, but I saw my grandparents, aunties, uncles, and cousins I had missed while trying to adjust to my other family who was far away from everybody. I missed all the family functions, celebrations, and gatherings I was used to. I missed going outside with my sisters and playing with our friends. I even missed being at church with everybody and getting into mischief with the church kids on the "other side" of the sanctuary. I realized that I didn't like it down in Georgia that much. And I couldn't really remember why until I returned years later when I was in middle school. My young mind totally removed myself from that experience, and my life went back to normal until the living in a shelter fiasco a few years later.

My daddy wasn't there for me when we lived in that shelter when I was a young child. It probably wasn't his fault. Regardless of who's to blame for that, it doesn't stop a little girl from feeling helpless in the pursuit to find love from a father figure, especially in hard times. I did not feel like a daddy was there protecting me how "they say" daddies are supposed to. That wouldn't be the end of my feeling unprotected by my father. Most girls who grow up in fatherless homes begin looking for love in all the wrong places as a result of not having that fatherly love, protection, provision, and affirmation they need daily. That started for me at a very young age, and it didn't stop for the next 10 years of my life to follow.

A few months after we moved into our two-family flat, my mama told me my daddy was coming to visit again. When my daddy pulled up in his truck, I was so shocked. I had no idea why he was coming to see me after all this time, but I felt excited, nonetheless. After spending the night with him and two of his younger daughters in a hotel, he asked me if I wanted to go back to Atlanta with him. This decision would be my choice, which was much different than that first time around. The fact that he asked me made me feel good that he considered me.

What I thought was a visit from my daddy, turned out to lead into a plan of actually moving again. It felt so wonderful to be around my daddy, plus I was receiving hugs from the loving arms I had longed for all my life, so I said yes. It didn't even cross my adolescent mind to think about all the loving family and friends I would be leaving behind yet again. I was imagining that life with him would be as blissful as that 24 hours spent together.

After returning to Atlanta, I was welcomed by my siblings Israel, Jireh, Tiyonna, Aniah, and new addition to the family, Halina. I believe they were 9, 8, 5, 4 and Halina was 1 and a half. Shortly after I settled into my daddy's house, we went to a family friend's house who had bags of clothes for me that were passed down from a girl my size who was out growing them. My daddy said that my mama sent me down there with too many dirty clothes, and he didn't want me wearing that stuff. That's when the whole "unlearning" began.

My daddy began frequently asking me questions about things I'd heard about him growing up, and who I thought he was because of that. Then with all the answers he didn't like, he began debunking the myths with counteractive stories about my mama and everything he wasn't allowed to do in the pursuit of trying to be a real father to me. It became so overwhelming and confusing at one point that I just stopped wanting to talk to him about those things.

We would have these conversations in the family room in front of my younger siblings and stepmom, and it was always uncomfortable. He would even ask me to share with everyone what it was like having to live in a shelter. I didn't like all these questions he would ask. I felt like the guinea pig example of how good my younger siblings had it, and how they should be grateful for a good life, living with both of their parents, all while having a stable roof over their heads. It stirred up a spirit of jealousy toward them.

My daddy also taught me a lot about myself that I didn't know. He taught me about how parents should take care of, provide for, and protect their children from hurtful life situations the best way they could. He also taught me how to take care of myself as a young girl who would one day become a young woman. He taught me how to cook. He taught me how to clean up a house from top to bottom, including doing laundry. He even taught me how to braid hair because he would often braid mine. Then I was given the task of helping out my stepmom with my little sisters' hair.

The learning kept going at a much faster rate than what I could keep up with sometimes. He assumed I wasn't taught much real respect for adults, so he and my stepmom began telling me all the things I could and could not say to them or other adults. They started making me call them sir and ma'am. I couldn't answer them when they called my name without saying "yes sir" or "yes ma'am." If I did, I would be punished. And their punishments weren't pleasant at all. I couldn't believe I had to change the way I talked, walked, looked, and felt all in such a short amount of time.

My daddy did so much teaching and trying to fix me from the person my mama had raised, that it was like he forgot I was his daughter and not his in-home student. Then when I wasn't learning the stuff fast enough or making mistakes along the way, that's when the whoopings and beatings started. The difference between a whooping and a beating are simple in my opinion. For me, a whooping is taking a belt, and spanking a child across the butt for doing something wrong that they knew was wrong to begin with. That is done in a way that the child feels the pain but doesn't have to receive medical attention for what they received.

A beating is when an angry person takes a belt, broomstick, pole, switch, cord, etc. and whoop a child, causing the child to feel a heightened level of excruciating pain. This results in the need of medical attention for the wounds they received in the process. I knew when my daddy or stepmom would whoop me, because my daddy would have loving group discussions to explain my wrongs and the reason for punishment shortly after. The beatings were different, and I always needed to go tend to wounds and welts on my skin afterwards. There was no talking after the beatings. Either they left the room, or I was told to exit immediately.

My daddy was a truck driver, so I was often left home with my stepmom and younger siblings for the majority of my stay. I remember him only being home 3 days out the week. Sometimes he was gone longer than a week. For me, I felt like I had come all this way to spend time with my daddy, only to have to spend it getting to know my stepmom and siblings instead. That was cool, but it wasn't my intent for moving. I appreciated the lessons I learned while he was home.

Whenever he wasn't home, I was almost always in trouble with my stepmom. She was so mean to me. It seemed as though she was always angry. I rarely saw her smile or laugh with me for anything. I don't know if her intentions for being that way toward me were to scare me into listening to her or what, but it worked. I was very afraid of her. She was emotionally, physically, and verbally abusive to me.

My stepmom often made me feel like the outsider around her. I remember when I turned 12 years old, she brought out my younger brother, Israel's, birthday cake to sing him happy birthday on my birthday. Israel's birthday was two whole weeks prior to mine. Yet we were all there surrounding his cake and singing to him like it was his day. I understand we were also poor in that house and they had to purchase cakes for everyone's birthday whenever they had the money, however celebrating his birthday on mine did not feel like a coincidence. My daddy didn't even say anything about it. I felt so hurt. And I'm sure my stepmom knew it.

Once I was able to cook, clean, and do laundry, I was doing those chores more frequently than everyone else. All the other kids were younger, so the responsibility often fell on me. It seemed as though my stepmom was beating me for every little thing at that point. If something wasn't cleaned, I was in trouble. If one of my siblings broke something, smeared feces all over the bathroom, or even wrote on the walls, I was in trouble too. She even beat me whenever one of my sibling's rooms wasn't clean no matter how well I kept up my own.

I couldn't quite understand why I was getting beaten for things I didn't do or had no ties to. Whenever my daddy would come home and hear about the stuff we got in trouble for, he explained that "teamwork makes the dream work." By that he meant if one of your rooms is dirty, then all of your rooms are dirty, and that meant we all got in trouble. However, I remember the main person in trouble each time being me.

This caused me to find outside relief in my friends at school and around the neighborhood. Any chance I had to be away from the house, I was taking it. However, I couldn't do a lot of the things my friends could do, besides go outside and play until the streetlights came on. And whenever I would want to venture off around the neighborhood, my stepmom said I had to take one of my little sisters with me. I often took little Halina because she was small enough to fit on my hip and couldn't talk to tell on me for anything I did out of the norm. Everybody knew that if I was coming, she was too. When I was allowed to be away from the house by myself, I was either exploring pure freedom and fun to the "next level" or up to no good with my friends. I wasn't a bad pre-teen, but I wasn't an angel either.

Although I was trying my best to make my stepmom happy at home, whatever I got in trouble for doing at school, I probably deserved the punishment. I attended Jean Childs Young middle school in Atlanta. I loved going to school because I used it as an outlet. I appreciated all the friends I gained while attending that middle school and cherished them like family. I loved them so much that I had an opportunity to go back home to Detroit after my sixth grade year ended., but I came back down to Atlanta instead just to be with them so we could go to seventh grade together. What a crazy decision that was.

When my seventh grade year started, it seemed like things at home grew worse. I second guessed my return to that place often. My stepmom was angrier more often and my daddy was gone a lot more. I would tell my daddy about the things that happened whenever he was gone, and to my knowledge, he didn't do anything about it. So, I stopped telling him. It came to the point where I was so afraid of my stepmom and trying my best to stay out of her way, that I couldn't even muster up the strength to ask her for feminine products during my times of the month. I remember becoming a great craftsman with the art of tissue, or just having to ask for things from friends whenever I was away from the house.

I endured my seventh grade year in Atlanta, and so much transpired that year at school for me. Once it was all over, I was ready to go back home to Detroit. I'm pretty sure my stepmom was ready for me to go back home as well. One day during that summer, my stepmom was dropping me off to dance practice at church. When we arrived, she started yelling at me about something I had done wrong at home. This yelling and verbal abuse was something I was so familiar with. So, I probably did roll my eyes like she said, but she still had no reason to do what happened next.

Before I could get out the door, she grabbed me by the throat and put her thumb in my windpipe to the point where I couldn't breathe. If she had choked me any longer than she did, I would be dead. She yelled, "Don't you ever roll your eyes at me again little girl! Do you hear me?" And when she finally let my neck go, I coughed and answered, "yes ma'am." I remember running straight to the church bathroom and crying there for a long time.

After that, I was walking on eggshells constantly. A few weeks after that incident, she started storming around the house mad about something. I don't know if something wasn't cleaned or what. I just know I couldn't take it anymore. I ran outside to my friend's house who stayed two doors down. I cried uncontrollably and told her I needed to use her phone. At my daddy's house I wasn't able to use the phone unless I asked first. After asking I had to let them know who I was calling and my reason for calling them. It was a lot. When my daddy was home, I would just ask him could I call so and so, and he would say yes. Asking my stepmom was when I got the third degree. That resulted in me rarely calling home to my mama and family in Detroit.

I only talked to them when they called for me, because I hated asking most times. However, this day I wasn't letting anything stop me. Once my friend gave me her phone, I dialed my mama's number and I believe my brother picked up. I started crying and told him that I needed to come home and how my step mama was always beating me, and how she even choked me once. I believe I was on speaker because I think I heard my mama say, she did what?

Next thing I know, my daddy was on his way home because my stepmom was receiving threats and voicemails from my brother and my people back home in Detroit about her putting her hands on me. One of the voicemails she played out loud in front of me, and I heard my big brother Kris' voice going off on her and telling her everything he would do to her when he saw her if she put her hands on me again. That was my first time feeling protected by a man. When I heard his voice, I felt excited and longed for someone to stand up for me like that.

When my daddy finally made it home, instead of getting mad at my stepmom he got mad at me. He told me how I was the wrong one for having them call his house with threats like that against his wife. I was so confused and felt like this was all my fault. Next thing I knew, we were having a meeting with the bishop at church. My daddy is a minister, so he had me in church just as much as my mama did when I lived in Detroit. However, I couldn't believe my daddy involved the bishop of this church.

When we went to the church office, this was the very first time I ever got to fully express all of my issues that were happening while my daddy was gone. The bishop agreed with how I was feeling. She told my stepmom she was wrong for doing what she did because she could have almost killed me. I was excited that the conversation was going in my favor until she looked at me in the eyes, and she said, "If you go back home to Detroit, you're going to have a baby. Specifically, a daughter." I don't know where she got this prophecy from, but I believed her with my whole heart, and my young 13-year-old self was nowhere near ready for kids. I had enough feeling like I was helping out too much with the siblings that weren't my children. That meeting scared me into staying another year.

During that summer we spent a lot of time in Tennessee with my stepmom's family. I'm assuming my stepmom needed a break from everything and everyone. It's pretty weird because her family loved on me like I was their own. They gave me things, taught me so much, and even shared stories about how they grew up. Her grandma, aunties, and cousins loved me way more than she ever did. We took a lot of family trips during the summer. Most of them were to Tennessee to see her family. When this particular summer was over, we came back home, and my daddy announced to us children that we were moving to Douglasville, outside of Atlanta. I was devastated.

I couldn't imagine living in Georgia without being close to the friends I loved so dearly. Staying connected to my neighborhood friends and school friends was the reason I had stayed when I had the chance to move back to Detroit. They were my outlets. They were my diaries. They were my good times and non stop laughter. They were the people who showed me the utmost affection. They were closer to me than the family I was living with. They were also where I was able to purely give and receive real love. I just knew my Georgia life was coming to an end. I spent one week of eighth grade with my friends before having to say my tearful and fearful goodbyes.

We moved to a house on a huge hill in Douglasville, Georgia. I was transferred a week and a half after school started to Chapel Hill Middle School. To my surprise this was a multiracial school. This was new for me. Growing up, I had been used to living in predominantly black neighborhoods and attending predominantly black schools. I didn't know how I was going to be able to adjust to this new life, all the while maintaining good graces at home.

As you can imagine, I kept my head down, my grades up, and my mind as sane as possible to make it through my entire eighth grade year.

By the time eighth grade was ending, I was so ready to go. I made a lot of great friends, and I still love them even to this day, but I could not take staying at the house anymore. That house was not a place of good memories. A lot happened there. Plus, it was as though I was on house arrest due to not being allowed to go anywhere. Over the course of my time there, I lost one of my favorite Sunday school teachers at church. Then we lost our beloved Grandma, my daddy's mom. Then my daddy was in a horrific truck accident and had to be in a neck brace for months. When he finally came home from the hospital, he and my stepmom took over my room because my bed was elevated higher than theirs, and he had to sleep in the neck brace.

During his down time my stepmom had to find a job. While she worked, every single responsibility that I had before had to be taken up a notch. If dinner wasn't already prepared by the time she came home, I was in trouble. I had to help with baths, homework, and even everybody's laundry. I began to feel like the housemaid. I was tired of cooking and cleaning for a whole house full of people. I remember feeling so overwhelmed to the point where I no longer wanted to be on earth anymore. I went to the bathroom one night, and held my breath in the tub to see how long it would take me to run out of breath and be out of here. After that attempt I realized what I was doing was stupid and I just needed to be honest with my daddy and tell him I needed to leave.

I didn't know how to break it to my daddy at first. What compelled me to actually tell him was one night we were all in his room getting yelled at about something. Then my stepmom came in with a broomstick. Every time my daddy asked me a question about whatever it was we were in trouble for, she hit me with the broom if I was answering too slow. I remember her hitting me 3 times because I was counting. Then I said this prayer in my head to God, "Lord if she hits me one more time, I am going to take that stick and beat the crap out of her. If you do not want that to happen, please don't let her hit me again."

After that prayer I stood there waiting patiently, bracing myself for how I was going to turn around and snatch the broomstick from her. Then my daddy let us go out of the room. She was saved. There was no telling how ugly that would have ended if she had hit me again. I believe I told my daddy the very next day I wanted to go home to Detroit, and he said okay. Shortly after that we found out my stepmom was pregnant again. I was so happy I was going home, because the last thing I wanted to do was be a maid for yet another person. A few weeks after eighth grade ended, I was on the first flight back home to Detroit.

How This Worked For Me

"When my father and mother forsake me, then the Lord will take care of me."

Psalm 27:10 (NKJV)

I didn't know if my daddy loved me before he started whooping and beating me. I didn't know how much he loved me before he let his wife beat me consistently. I believe it hinders our relationship with God when we don't receive proper love and protection from our fathers. Loving my daddy came naturally to me when I first found out who he was. But in return, I didn't know how to receive love from him or even understand if love was supposed to be the way he was teaching it.

In my daddy's house, I learned that you are punished for what you do wrong. No amount of love can make you feel safe or protected even in your mess. Grace did not reside there. But from what the Bible says, God's love isn't like that. It's the total opposite. It's unconditional. It's unwavering. It causes grace and mercy to be activated in and through our lives no matter what we've done. I don't think there is anything wrong with correcting a child's behavior. I believe when punishment outweighs the love you show, then there comes the problem.

The blessing that this situation brought me was learning the nature of forgiveness. Since my daddy and stepmom are one through marriage, I had to forgive them both. First, I had to throw out all the ideas of what life with them was supposed to be for me and accept how it was. I had to come to terms with the idea that maybe that's how they were raised, and that was all they knew. My mama didn't raise me the way they were teaching. The frequent chastisement was abuse in my eyes because of the major transition. My daddy tried to change me so much in just a few short years of finally being able to be with him, and I couldn't keep up. I had to have an open heart to let go of these things because bitterness was growing inside of me daily.

Forgiving my daddy was easy. I just knew that I would always love him no matter what because he is my daddy. I realized that my whole life living with him wasn't that bad. We had a lot of great times and we shared a lot of laughs and great memories. I could only view my experience there through the eyes of my pain because it was way louder than my joyful moments there. Once I finally pushed past my emotions, I was able to let him know how I felt all those years.

The issue showed up when I realized I had to forgive my stepmom as well. For years that was something that I thought I could never do. As I grew closer to God, I recognized that I had to forgive her because He forgave me. I tried just saying "I forgive her" for 5 years straight. However, every time I would see her on my daddy's social media or in person, those old feelings would creep back up again.

Forgiveness is a full-blown surgery. It's not a simple doctor visit to the office of the Lord where He checks your heart rate, then approves you to go home. No, it is an internal operation that starts with your heart and transfers to your spirit. It is then followed up with a prescription for total healing. You have to do some intense work.

I had to sit in those feelings and allow myself to feel every single part of them without running away or distracting myself. When anger rose up in me and sobbing cries met me, I had to fully embrace them. Then I had to unpack all of my feelings in order to gain some type of understanding. After the understanding, I had to let each feeling go one by one. It didn't matter that each feeling was left without an apology of their own. I had to let it go. That is release and freedom from what people have done to you. It is a tough process, but it is so worth it.

Forgiveness helped me to actually build a real relationship with my daddy. Our relationship has grown tremendously. He started to surprise me and show up at my dorm or apartment at least once every year while I was in college. Since I've moved to L.A., he randomly pops up to see me during his truck routes. Although I don't see him often, most of our relationship is rebuilt through communication over the phone. We are closer now than what I could have ever imagined if I didn't push past my hurt.

We can now talk about everything under the sun. He gives me advice on different relationships. He has helped me navigate complicated situations. He has taught me so much about God. He actually lets me vent and release all of my frustrations and sorrows when necessary. And sometimes he calls me just to tell me that he loves me and he's proud of me. Not to mention he texts me poems whenever he writes them, and I think that is the sweetest thing ever.

Whenever he pops up in town, we stay up all night long talking until he falls asleep on me or vice versa. I laugh uncontrollably every time I'm in his presence because he's so funny to me. Whenever we haven't seen each other or spoken in a while, he leaves me beautifully heartfelt voicemails if I miss his call. These are things that make my love for him grow daily. It brings healing to every part of my heart that longed for these things growing up. Once I forgave him and opened my heart to what God wanted to do in our relationship, I was able to see him in a new way.

Chapter Three

Mama Issues Work

I always wondered what a mother's love was supposed to be like, feel like, and look like. From the things I've seen in life, a mother's love is the strongest love out there next to God's love for us. I can't really give my point of view for what a mother's love should be due to me not having children yet. I can't tell whether the love from a mother is coming out wrong, or if it's supposed to be gentle, thoughtful, and caring. I can however explain this love from a daughter's point of view. Loving our mamas comes easily. It's like opening your eyes first thing in the morning while waking up. You don't think about it, you just do it. So, whenever you find it difficult to open your eyes, then you know that you have a problem.

I realized I had a problem when I would say things like, "My mama care more about the church than she cares about me." Or "My mama doesn't do stuff for me like that." Or "Why can't my mama be more like their mama?" or "How come when I ask my mama for help, she don't ever have any money?" Or "How come I didn't get a mama who was willing to go all out for her kids with everything?" These thoughts and questions led me to believe that I had problems with my mama that were too deep to resolve by myself. I needed divine intervention in order to fix these issues. These were wounds too deep for me to cover with a bandage. I needed some stitching done in my heart.

In chapter one, *Growing Pains*, I explained quite a bit of what led me to this growing up. I honestly blamed my mama for all of it. I blamed her for the filthy home we grew up in. I blamed her for the way we went to school with dirty clothes on at times. I blamed her for the hardship of having to live in a homeless shelter. I blamed her for my life's struggle with stability for years to follow. Once I started playing the blame game in my relationship with my mama, then it was easy for me to be upset with her for everything else.

I've known all my life that my mama loves me. There was no doubt there. What I questioned was her full ability to show it. I knew my mama loved me when she would always put her face against mine and rub our noses together when I was a little girl. And whenever she would hold my hand all the way to school and not let go until I was officially in my classroom. It wasn't until I started growing and witnessing other mamas do things for my friends that my mama wouldn't do or never did. I believe comparison played a big part in whatever it was that made me feel cold inside when it came to my mama. There were also things on her part that I think could have been done better to prevent that as well.

My mama's love for church made me want to know who God really was. When I was younger, I didn't quite understand how someone could be so in love with God that they make it their business to serve His house no matter what. Even if the home they were living in was crumbling. When I was a child my focus wasn't on God, my focus was on my mama and who I knew she was supposed to be to me. I started noticing that she spent more time at the church than she spent at home. When she started to leave us home while she went to church, it created a disconnect of communication in our home. I don't remember ever sitting down having conversations with our mama and being able to share things happening to us or around us. If she wasn't at church, she was at work. Then when she stopped working, it was all church from there on out. I recognize now that having a love for church and having a love for God are two totally different things.

One day at church, I saw that my mama was giving away money or candy to kids when they brought their report cards to her. She would give them these gifts for every A or B they had. I had been a straight A student most of my life and never remembered being rewarded for my academics the way she was rewarding them. At that very moment, even though I was young, I knew that planted a bad seed in me toward my mama. And I later began to associate it with the phrase, "my mama likes the church kids more than she likes me." Church kids loved my mama, and probably still do to this day. They were always able to come to her and talk to her about anything. I didn't have those same experiences. I never dwelled on that too much growing up, but I know it played a part in my bitterness toward her later on.

We would also have shut-ins at the church on certain weekends where all the kids and a few adults spent the night at church playing games while learning about Jesus. The age groups were always separated. Ages 9 and below were in the back or "on the other side" for us. And the ages 10 and up were in the sanctuary. The age groups were then separated into smaller sections within the area of the church they were in. On one of those shut-in occasions, I snuck out from the back and hid under the pews where teenagers were.

My mama and another adult from the church were talking to the teens about sex, I'm guessing. I assumed because of a phrase

I overheard from my mama. I peeked from under the pew to listen, because I could hear my mama's voice. She was looking at the group and she said the words, "when I was 16, I used to love sex." I was only 9 years old at the time, but I knew that was a conversation I was not supposed to be a part of. So, I crawled under the pews to another section where other teens were, and this section was more fun because I was watching them play games. Those words that my mama shared with those teenagers didn't pop back up in my head until *I* was 16 and struggling with promiscuity. When I remembered it, I felt upset. I wondered why she never had conversations with me like that to prevent me from going down the same path, as I'm sure she did with them. How come she never had the "sex talk" with me? That is a question I asked myself during the times of my struggle.

When Aunty Kesha came to pick us up before the shelter fiasco, my mama wasn't there. Aunty Kesha was pretty upset at that, and it was her main reason for taking us in for the summer. As I mentioned in chapter one, she washed our clothes, did our hair and took us to school as frequently as she could for the rest of the semester. My mama had done these same things for us before, and for the majority of our lives. I'm not sure how we ended up looking as if we were neglected. Maybe at that time, Aunty Kesha saw something we as children didn't see. All I know is that when someone would ask me where my mama was, church was the best and most accurate answer I could give.

After the time I spent living with my dad in middle school, I realized everything I knew how to do as it pertains to taking care of myself and keeping up a home was all taught by him. I often wondered where the ball was dropped on my maternal end, however comparing the two was not something I ever liked to do. I also realized that spending that time down in Atlanta played a huge part in my disconnect in communication as well. Since I was fearful of using the phone as much as I wanted to, I depended on people calling me in order for me to talk to them. As much as you would think a mother would contact her daughter, my mama didn't call me much at all. I had no motherly figure to nurture and sooth my wounds and sorrows with anything I was experiencing during that time.

When I came back home to Detroit, my mama was the first person I was happiest to see. I just knew with our time apart, she missed me as much as I missed her. I arrived home during the summertime, so I didn't expect my mama to be at the church every day for the summer, but she was. She had found a new church home by the time I returned, but her time spent there was way more than the time spent in the church I grew up in.

I was familiar with this particular church because my Aunty Kesha attended this church before I left home. I don't know the change of events that occurred for my mama's transfer, but I did know she was way more comfortable with these people than the last. From what I knew, she was there often because she was working there. She managed the summer Bible school they had there at the time. I went with her as often as I could until I got tired of it and was completely over hanging with the few people my age who were there.

Coming home, I realized there was a change in our living location as well. My mama and siblings were no longer living in the two-family flat we moved into after the shelter. This house was a different two-family flat that we had all to ourselves. However, my mama had a member from the church and her older son living with us as well. I found out through my sisters that my family was evicted from the previous place. My Aunty Kesha ended up coming to pick us up again because my mama went out of town with the church and left us at home alone. We were all teens at the time, so we could take care of ourselves. The issue was my mama's friend was gone as well, but her 18-year-old son was not.

It wasn't too long after going to Aunty Kesha's house that my family was being evicted and seeing our things put out on the street again. This time my mama went to the homeless shelter by herself, and my aunty took my sisters and me in. So much happened with that situation and it really made me want to just give up on believing that life could get any better. I remember my aunty and my mama getting into an outrageous argument. My big brother got involved as well, then it turned into a catastrophe. This led my mama to the kitchen where she grabbed a knife, held it close to her wrist, and said that she was about to just kill herself. My big sister and I ran to grab the knife out of her hand. She kept grabbing it and it wasn't until my big brother came into the kitchen that she finally let it go.

Talk about trauma. That was one of the most disturbing things I had yet to witness. I was so hurt. I couldn't believe it. Although she didn't go through with the suicide attempt, I couldn't help but feel like something had already died inside of me. I knew she had to be going through a tough battle, but I still blamed her for that feeling I was feeling. But now I realize how inconsiderate I was to not look at all of the hurt she was going through, while her children wanted no part of it. We didn't want to go to the shelter with her that time. And I could only imagine how lonely she felt while being there.

After she left the homeless shelter, we ended up living with my older brother in his studio apartment. I felt so ashamed. My freshman year of high school was around this time, and I was meeting new friends, and having to make up stories about the "house" that I lived in. I eventually told my ninth grade best friend toward the end of the school year, and she didn't judge me one bit like I thought people would. Now I regret my shame and wish I had been more grateful for a roof over my head.

We went from that studio with my older brother to a one bedroom apartment he ended up renting not too far from mama's church. It was also close to the beauty shop my aunty was doing hair in. That's when I started working at the shop part-time as my aunty's assistant. By the time my mama finally rented her own house, I had already gone to live with my aunty again. I didn't trust that my mama would be able to keep the new big house she had just moved to, so for a while I stayed with my aunt and just went to school from there. It wasn't until I got into some trouble at my aunt's house that I moved back in with my mama. At that time, I really didn't have any choice. I did realize that my mama had the house since my sophomore year of high school and I was approaching my junior year, so I gave the time some credit and kept the faith. Living in that house actually lasted two years.

On the day before my 18th birthday, heartbreak struck again. All I could think was, "This can't possibly be happening to me. I am about to turn 18 years old tomorrow, and I am sitting here watching all of my stuff get put out on the street *again*." Luckily my mama had time to prepare and call a moving truck to come move our things. We ended up going to some project apartments on the deep eastside of Detroit that were abandoned and filled with bed bugs. My arms and back would be completely covered in bug bites and itching terribly every day.

I cried myself to sleep for the whole two or three days that I had to stay there until my aunty took me back in. It was horrible. Not to mention there were shootings all the time in that area. People were dying so close to us every night. Shortly after settling in, the apartment was broken into and they robbed us of everything valuable. Enough was enough. I was disappointed in my mama yet again for us having to live like this.

I wanted to be nothing like my mama during that time in my life. I hated her inability to keep a roof over our heads. I hated how much time she spent at that church. I realized they never supported her at all during our down times. I couldn't understand why she chose to continue supporting them faithfully every single day. I hated the fact that I could never ask her for any help financially. I couldn't believe that she wasn't able to help me with prom, graduation, or my send off to college. She didn't even travel with us when it was time for me to go. I hated the fact that she wasn't there for me whenever I needed her the most.

It wasn't until I went to college that I realized how much a mother is supposed to mean to you. I would sit around and watch my college friends talk to their mothers every day on the phone. I didn't understand it at all. I talked to my mama once every 6 months or so, and it didn't faze me. The majority of my friends would've had a heart attack if they spent two days without talking to their mamas. For me, I just thought that if she didn't call me, then she probably didn't want to talk, and I was okay with that for a moment. Plus, we never had any conversations past the surface level of "how you doing" and "what you doing," and I was tired of that.

I would talk to my aunty all the time though, and think that was enough for me, but deep down inside, I really needed to feel that love and care from my mama that I witnessed from other girls and their moms. Meeting all my friends' moms in person and seeing their love, support, care, encouragement, provision, and guidance made me feel sad. I would often cry about it in my alone time. So I began to reevaluate my resentment, blame, and feelings of neglect.

How This Worked For Me

"Honor your father and mother," which is the first commandment with promise: "that it may be well with you and you may live long on the earth."

Ephesians 6:2-3 (NKJV)

I believe the seeds of disappointment and discontentment were planted in me to dishonor my mama. Not honoring your parents cuts your days short on earth. I couldn't let my issues with my mama stand in the way of me honoring her and who she is in my life. I had a very selfish method of coming up with all the things I blamed my mama for. I didn't realize that my mama was actually going through those things we went through too. I was under the impression that she was supposed to be some type of "shero" to protect me from life's trials because she was all I had for a while. I was just experiencing the effects of whatever her trials were because I was there. We went through a lot together, although I felt alone.

Everybody struggles differently. Everyone expresses love differently as well. My mama gave love the best way she knew how. I had to come to terms with the fact that love for children is not always about what you can and can't do for them. And I had to understand that church was probably an outlet my mama used to cope with all the trials that have taken place in her life through poverty, trauma, and health issues. I won't tell her story, but I will say that I know she has been through a lot in her life. My expectations of her were just something she couldn't fulfill. And as long as I keep the command to honor her, God will supply everything else I need.

I never took into consideration the way she fought through health issues to even seem like a normal parent for us. All I could see was what I wasn't getting because of what other kids were getting around me. I thought what I saw in my friends' relationships with their moms was the norm and that my mama wasn't normal. That's why comparison is the thief of joy. Had I taken my eyes off other people and the way I thought things "should have been," I would have noticed that my mama was doing the best with the cards she had been dealt. And yes, there are always areas for growth, but who am I to judge the way she processes and deals with life when she's been dealt a tough hand? I needed a change in my perspective.

My mama did indeed bless my life to know Jesus. The greatest gift she could've ever given me in life was presented to me at birth. From then on, my mama has not ceased to display and mention her love and devotion to the Father through her service to Him and His people. She taught me that no matter what you go through in life, and no matter where life takes you, if you find yourself in the hands of Jesus, then you are good to go. She taught me what it means to be an overcomer. She has overcome so much and never gave up on God. I'm not sure what gave her that kind of strength, but I am sure that she passed it right along to me, and for that I am forever grateful.

Honoring our parents is for us, not them. We won't always understand what they have going on in their worlds, but we have to trust God to see us through it as a whole. The minute we take our eyes off of God in the dealings of any parental relationship, we lose sight of the blessing that it is to even still have that parent in our lives. Yes, it may not be the best relationship, but each day that both of us are blessed with breath is another chance for growth. Seeking God in that area works. It's so much easier said than done, I know. I also know the trauma and turmoil we go through in our emotions with unbalanced parental relationships can play out into our relationships with others.

Since having the conversation with my mama about rebuilding a better relationship, things have changed drastically. She never ceases to support me in everything I do. She always lets me know that I have made her proud in life, and that is my greatest desire fulfilled every time. I believe that once my perspective was changed, the posture of my heart changed. And after continual prayer about all of this, God has shown up. I didn't give up hope that our relationship could grow. God has done that and more with the both of us. If mama issues were never a thing for me, I would not have gotten the chance to experience this level of glory.

Chapter Four

Crummy Secrets Work

When I was in second grade, my sisters and I attended Colin Powell Academy. It was our very first charter school experience, and we noticed they did things a little differently than the normal Detroit public schools. Every week we had an assembly of some sort in our school's auditorium. They would be teaching us songs, reciting the pledge of allegiance, and giving us the agenda and announcements for the school week. Sometimes they had presentations sharing random pieces of information with us that we as students didn't know we needed. One day, we had an assembly presentation that was a little longer than usual. A group of people dressed in weird costumes came into the auditorium and started performing different skits about our bodies for us. All the kids were laughing, and it seemed to be very entertaining at first. These skits were weird to me at the moment, but they soon brought on a sense of shame by the time it was over.

I can't remember all of the characters that were on stage that day or everything they presented specifically. I do remember someone dressed up in a huge cookie costume. And there was a woman narrating the story lines. She began first pointing out all of the different "private areas", where our "private parts" were located on our bodies. After explaining that these areas were private, she began calling them cookies. The huge cookie was standing in front of the stage when out of nowhere, one of the other characters came up and touched the cookie on the butt. The cookie jumped up and we as students had to repeat after the narrator saying, "No, no, no, you can't touch my cookie." The cookie ran to the nearest adult to tell what the other character had done. Then the narrator explains to us that if anyone was to ever touch any of us in those cookie areas, we are to say no, and go and tell the nearest adult. Before closing out the presentation she looked at all of us and said, "Don't keep *Crummy Secrets*!" While simultaneously rubbing her fingers together on both hands as if to create the imaginary crumbs from the cookie. Then we had to repeat after her saying, "Don't keep *Crummy Secrets*!" I didn't know at the time that this presentation was specifically safety lessons for child sexual abuse prevention. I did know that by that time in my life, this presentation was just a little too late.

Keeping crummy secrets was already a practice I had gotten used to. I didn't understand the importance or magnitude of such a conversation to have with children until I became an adult. The secrets I kept weren't intentional secrets. I believe I just didn't know how to tell or speak out loud whatever it was that I experienced. Feelings of shame and dirtiness always crept over me at the thought of telling anybody whenever I was being touched by someone. After experiencing this kind of touching with other children, I thought it was normal. Everybody was touching everybody by that time. Some of it I saw with my own eyes, and most of it was happening to me firsthand. When I look back on it, other kids were touching me, because somebody else was touching them.

I was roughly 5 or 6 years old around the time I experienced my first "touch." We would go over to family's homes as kids to spend the nights and have longer stays if it was summertime. I remember being over at a family member's house, and we as kids were often left at home to be watched by an extended family member of the house I was at. Let's just say, this man was no kin to me. I guess that's what made him feel okay with whatever he did. I was lying down on a bed one day taking a nap. It was daylight. I remember having on jean shorts. I woke up just a little to realize that my shorts had been unbuttoned, unzipped, and there this man was sitting on the bed next to me with his hand pulling up my shorts. I turned over to pretend I was stretching to go back to sleep. While lying on my stomach, I could feel his hand underneath the rim of my shorts. He was rubbing the back of my thigh right under my butt cheek. As his fingers swayed back and forth, I had never felt so dirty in my life. There was also a tingly feeling that started happening in my vagina as I laid there. I kept my face turned and pretended to still be asleep until he left.

I didn't know what to do, who to tell, or even what to ask the man who had just left the room. I believe I even had to readjust my underwear before fastening my shorts back up. I don't know what exactly happened to me that day. I don't remember the sequence of events that led up to me waking up and realizing he was there. I can only assume that my sleep was deep enough to protect my young mind from experiencing the full time of his presence. I can't recall what happened later on that night or any time after that. What I know for sure is that after that day that tingly feeling in my vagina never went away. And for some odd reason I desired whatever it was I was feeling to be cured by another touch of some sort.

The next crummy secret I kept was something I thought I would never tell to this day. As I mentioned before, kids were touching each other almost every time adults weren't around. I don't know who is to blame for all we experienced growing up, but I do believe these kids weren't doing this out of nowhere. It mainly happened when boys and girls were left together unattended. I remember my first kiss ever happened at age 7 with a boy who was 2 years older than I was. And we were around a group of kids who were all kissing each other as well because we got left in a basement while all the parents were upstairs having some type of gathering. It may have been Bible study. It was with church friends for sure. It was our first time having been left around young boys and I guess they just knew what to do. We had a lot of sleepovers with friends from church that were always safe as long as there were no big brothers, cousins, or uncles around.

However, this crummy secret changed my viewpoint on gender roles in this area. A large group of church girls went on a trip somewhere. I was roughly 9 years old. I can't remember where we went, but I don't remember seeing boys there. There were so many of us and the age range was from about 8 to 18. We had to spread out and sleep in different areas of the hotel, which included kitchens, bathrooms, etc. We had a few chaperones, but no one was watching us during bedtime. There was a girl who had obviously been more advanced in the "touching" area than myself. That night, we kissed. But not only did she kiss me, she touched me. I had no idea what she was doing touching me down there until the tingly feeling I had been wondering about since I was 5 had disappeared from a new feeling of satisfaction. I immediately stopped everything and went to the bathroom.

Although this new weird thing that happened to me felt good at the time, I never wanted to be touched by a girl again. The feelings of shame and being dirty crept over me the same way it did when I was 5 and in that room with that grown man sitting over me. I felt scared. I didn't know what was happening to me or what to think. It wasn't until later that I realized she had introduced me to masturbation. I could never blame this young girl for what I had experienced or how I felt disgusted at the thought of her ever touching me again. All I could wonder was who taught her that? Who touched her in that way to where she knew what to do? We were the same age. I felt so confused. I left that trip throwing what happened to the back of my head. It wasn't until that tingly feeling showed up again, that I began to practice what I had learned.

This last crummy secret is one I wish I could take back, but I can't because it happened. In the seventh grade, while living with my dad, I had a crush on a teacher. I don't know where it came from or how it happened honestly. I just know that he was a man who listened, comforted, made me laugh, and showed me the love I wasn't receiving back home while my daddy was gone, and my stepmom was in her angry season. As I mentioned in *Daddy Issues*, most girls who grow up in fatherless homes begin looking for love in all the wrong places as a result of not having that fatherly love, protection, provision, and affirmation they need daily. This situation was one of my many "wrong places." Although I was now living with my daddy, he was still gone a lot of the time, and I didn't know how to receive the kind of love he was dishing out. I didn't feel protected by him at all with anything I was enduring there. And I was punished for my wrongs more than I was affirmed in my accomplishments or who I was.

Everything I thought I needed in a manly figure, this man was. I was only 13 years old, and I know now that I never really knew what I wanted or needed back then. I wasn't dating yet or involved with any of the boys in my grade during this time, so my attraction to this grown man was all that I could see. I remember skipping lunches and lingering around a little after school just to be in his classroom laughing at his jokes and talking about all the students who did crazy things. One day I cried about something going on at home, and he was there to comfort me about it. In that same instance, I expressed my deep like for him. He completely shut me down and told me how forbidden it was because of our age difference and the fact that he was my teacher. He even told me I would make a wonderful wife and some man would be a happy husband to me one day. I don't know why, but that kind of affirmation only made me want to continue liking him in the way that I shouldn't.

Two weeks before the school year was out, I guess he gave in. One day while I was with him during my lunch hour, he closed the classroom door, shut the blinds to the windows, then sat me on his lap at his desk. He told me how beautiful I was and how much he loved my lips. Then he kissed me. Since I had kissed boys before, I knew how to kiss him back, and that prompted the question to follow. He asked me if I was a virgin. I immediately told him no because I liked the feeling of being in his arms, and I didn't want him to think I was lame. I was lying big time and hoping deep down that he never found out. He gave me his email and told me to contact him whenever I got home, and he would figure out a way for us to be together outside of school.

Every day after that, I would spend my lunch hours with him, and we would kiss. Once I felt comfortable enough, I let him touch and kiss my breast. I guess the kissing and touching was supposed to progress further, so one day he revealed himself to me. That was my first time ever seeing a man that close and personal. Before anything could happen, we were saved with a knock at the door. It was another teacher who needed him and wondered why I wasn't at lunch with all my other classmates. Later that day I shared what I saw and experienced with a friend. He had told me plenty of times before to keep what we had between us, but after the revealing, I just needed to let that out to somebody. I'm not sure if it was the friend I told or the teacher that came to the door in question, but by the time I got home that day, the principal or someone important from school was calling my house.

When I returned to school after the call, I remember him looking at me with anger and disgrace telling me that I was messing up his life. Although that hurt my feelings, I still cared about him. So, I lied to every adult who ever asked me what had happened between us. I lied to teachers, I lied to the assistant principal and counselors, and yes, I lied straight to my daddy and my stepmom's faces. I just knew those two would try to kill me if they knew the truth. I deleted emails and ripped up pages in my diary that expressed every way he made me feel. I denied my lunch whereabouts and anything else people questioned.

My attempts to protect him with my crummy secret didn't work. He was missing from class on the last two days of school. I just knew it was my fault. I was down about it for a very long time. The hurt I felt over the situation felt like heartbreak, anxiety and every emotional rollercoaster at the "in my feelings" theme park. I was mainly very confused. I later recognized that I was having withdrawals from an unhealthy attachment I created while trying to fill the abandonment voids I had in my heart. My views on the way men looked at young girls had been destroyed since age 5. I didn't think what my teacher was doing was normal. I just never thought I would be an enabler to such a physically and mentally harmful decision.

How This Worked For Me

"Behold, I give you the authority to trample on serpents and scorpions, and over all the power of the enemy, and nothing shall by any means hurt you."

Luke 10:19 (NKJV)

First and foremost, I do not in any way condone the things mentioned above at all. Stating that this "worked for me" is a declaration of the new knowledge, perspective and healing I have gained for this area of my life with the help of God. Sexual abuse to minors is a topic not often discussed openly, and if it takes my story to be the stance against such darkness, then I am more than willing to enter the fight. Exposing the enemy's tactics is the only way to know where to hit first.

Molestation and pedophilia are evil spirits the enemy uses to attack and destroy both the victim and the guilty in a lot of families. If this is never addressed and punished in the light, then it can become a generational curse that continues. After realizing that I was not alone in this, I had to be honest with myself about how it has affected me and my life. I believe that if I stay silent about my truth then it robs others of being able to fully face theirs.

In 2018 I asked God to show me where the root of lust came from in my life. I had been dealing with so much mentally and physically because of it. I had struggles with masturbation and pornography after being sexually abstinent for almost 3 whole years by that time. Although my abstinence continues, at that point I was about to give up. I was tired of dealing with my urge to go back to a sexually impure lifestyle. I was well on my way to satisfy the urge when I finally submitted it to God in prayer. I went on a fast and He began to show me the things I explained in this chapter. These were things I had forgotten about for so long. That first touch at 5 years old was the root to perversion entering my life, and it went on from there.

When I first started remembering what happened to me while being young, I couldn't stomach it for a long time. It wasn't until I finally expressed it in a therapy session, that I was able to tell what I remember out loud. I have not yet completed my therapy process with this area of my life, but I know that this thing no longer has a hold on me. I was able to uproot the spiritual bondage it had me in through prayer and fasting.

Not only did I attack it from the root in my spirit, but I also broke the curse and covenants it had with my family. When Jesus said we would have the power to trample on "snakes and scorpions," He was talking about emblems of demonic powers. Older men and women touching minors is demonic. There is no other way to describe that kind of evil. The guilty have allowed the influence of those evil spirits to take over their minds and infiltrate their victims. The victims have no idea what has been done to them spiritually until the effects of it plays out in their lives and relationships. There are some families who want to pretend these things don't happen, but you miss the opportunity to shine light on darkness when you ignore such things.

We have the power to win over the enemy's devices against us and our children (future children for me). There is no way young girls and boys should know how to touch each other unless they witness it or experience someone doing that to them. Talk to children. Ask them questions. Create safe spaces in your homes for children to feel secure in sharing their experiences with honesty. Teach them the places of their bodies that are off limits to others at an early age. Keep children out of homes of people you don't know. Interview everybody when it comes to your kids, especially the adults you send them to school with.

Parents can enroll into sexual abuse prevention programs that include safety training. Always seek help from wise and reliable counselors on this subject if you struggle with it. Make no assumptions that everything is okay with your children all the time. Take over this area with the power and authority Jesus has given us. We do that through prayer, fasting, knowledge, protection, honesty, therapy, preventative measures, increasing security, and serving justice to the guilty.

Chapter Five

Mistakes Work

Making mistakes in life seems to come easier to me than tying my shoe. Who would've thought that when God put us here on the earth, doing the wrong thing would become so common? It's so common that God is often blamed for something happening to us. Most times it was the very mistakes we made on our own that brought us there. I don't have enough fingers to count on to express how many mistakes I have already made in my lifetime. There are some mistakes I never thought I would see the end to the consequences of. The only thing I have always been sure of is that, when you fail, God is right there to pick up all of the pieces. I spent a lot of times praying and crying about things that I put myself right in the middle of. A lot of my greatest mistakes have happened during my struggle with promiscuity.

At age 14, I got a lot of "talking to" about sex. Before I left my dad's house, he would say that sex is good, however you need to wait until you're married to do it. In the church we learned a little about soul ties created from sex, but I guess that stuff didn't resonate with me, and I sure didn't retain the information well. When I arrived back home in Detroit, I had older cousins who would talk about it, saying they wish they had waited. The reason being was to save it for that special someone. None of them ever mentioned waiting until marriage.

On the other hand, I had plenty of friends who were already active, but most of them weren't sharing the full details of the experience. I just knew they enjoyed it and were doing it frequently. I came to the conclusion that it was some kind of mystery that was too good for the wrong person, too bad before marriage, and too cool not to act on now. Honestly all the cross talk and confusion made me curious. Plus, the way my hormones were set up, I wanted to know what was beyond the usual "second base" experiences I already had before.

That summer my experiments took me to a third base level when I was left home alone with the guy who was 18 years old. This was the guy I mentioned in *Mama Issues* when my mama and her friend/roommate went out of town. This guy was well experienced and had kids to show for it. Although I was initially enticed, it was my curiosity that agreed to go through with it. The fourth base didn't work out on my end because of the discomfort. Unfortunately, my whole family found out about my experience when Aunty Kesha read the text messages I sent to a friend. She told everybody.

Next thing I knew she and my Aunty Te Te were taking me to get a pregnancy test. I still don't know where that idea came from. The crazy thing is my hymen was still intact, and unless I was Mary, there was no way a pregnancy test would've been positive. That wasn't the end of the fiasco. Once my older brother found out, he went to my mama's church and beat up the guy who was responsible for the experience. This situation made me want to sneak and hide everything I did moving forward. I was going to do my thing without telling nobody nothing! That idea worked for a while, until it all came crashing down.

Upon entering the ninth grade at Northwestern High School, I found that there were a lot of guys who found me attractive. I would hear guys call me all types of names all day long trying to get my attention. They would say, "come here *girl*, *baby*, *boo*, *beautiful*, *fine a**, sexy*," and whatever clever name they could think of. Some of these guys were so dumb, they would just say, "aye big booty girl! I know you hear me calling you! Aye girl with the big booty!" It was outrageous and hilarious all at the same time. I ignored it most of the time. However, hearing it was flattering until they started acting disrespectful when I didn't acknowledge them.

That kind of attention was different from anything I had ever experienced in middle school. It made me feel wanted. It made me feel seen. It validated places inside of me that I had never experienced before. I knew that I was growing into my figure and all the places a woman can develop had already begun on me. I took pride in the way my shape was turning out. I knew guys liked that about me. I began to feel like I was coming alive. As if I had been in a shell my entire life and now, I was finally being recognized for the butterfly that I am.

One of those guys calling at me must have said something worth hearing, because the next thing I knew, I had a boyfriend by the end of my first semester in high school. And I got into plenty of fights and arguments at the school trying to keep him. He was a senior and I was a freshman. Some of my people thought he was too old for me, but I used to always claim an unhealthy liking of "older guys" anyway. This was my first real boyfriend. I thought I was so deep in love that I would never come out of it. My love for him made it easy for us to enter the fourth base world pretty quickly, and before I knew it, I was skipping school to go have sex. That was common among my friends at Northwestern. I actually learned a lot from them. Everybody I was friends with was already active and had plenty of answers to whatever questions I had. That was the birth of my promiscuity journey.

I proceeded to fully indulge in that area of promiscuity during that time in my life. It led me to lying, cheating in relationships, sneaking, and repeating these same mistakes. By the tenth grade I transferred to Detroit School of Arts, and although I was at a new school, and newly single, I still had all of my old habits. I would skip school on Fridays to go be with the person I left my old boyfriend for. I was a complete mess by then. I was in search of some type of feeling that I couldn't quite put my finger on. If someone wasn't fulfilling the need I had, then I was on to the next adventure with no remorse. This craving and seeking behavior was very detrimental to my life. I had no idea how bad it was until it turned scary.

I made the biggest mistake ever when I started sneaking my partners in the house at night. I didn't want anyone to know what I was doing, but my search for this unquenchable thirst I had was crucial. By the time I came up with this idea, tenth grade was over, and it was already summertime. I couldn't skip school anymore because school was out. My aunty knew exactly where I was all day, every day because I worked at the hair salon as her assistant.

With all of that into consideration, the nighttime was my only way to try and find relief of the burning desire that was plaguing me. I don't even remember how I was sleeping at night because this scheme was so crazy. I was only involved with one person at the time, and we had a routine going that seemed to work perfectly. We got into a big argument, and he didn't want to come over anymore. My desire hadn't stopped, so I needed another option. This is when it turned dangerous.

I started meeting guys everywhere on the block, at the shop, or even in random corner stores. I was giving out my number like I was promoting a business while trying to scout out my next fix. Guys never hesitated to holler out to me or say cute things to get my attention. They even stopped in their cars and pulled up alongside me offering me rides whenever I was walking down the street. I wasn't taking any of those rides. However, to know that I was desirable to different guys was gratifying. I saw how easy it would be to fulfill the longings I had of being touched.

It wasn't long before I took a liking to someone new. This man actually made an effort to approach me with sweet words. He stopped his car, got out and walked over to me on the way to the store one day. He told me he was only 19 after he found out I was 16. I thought that was cool because "older guys were my thing." This guy also had his baby in the car, so I assumed he was pretty harmless.

Turns out the guy was a stalker. I had no idea at first because he was so sweet. We talked on the phone and texted all day and night for at least two weeks. By that time, I was more than ready for some fourth base action because that's all I wanted from him to begin with. I had a list of guys that I created. I was ready to move on to whoever was next in line, but this guy wanted to know more about me every day. He started taking up my time on the phone that I could've have spent assessing my next guy.

Then he started asking for pictures of me. Not just any pictures, it was the very inappropriate ones. I would always tell him no every time he asked. Then one day he did something nice for me, and I thought I owed it to him as a reward for his nice gesture. So, I sent the pictures he asked for. After that, he started plotting how we would get together for our fourth base appointment. I didn't delay letting him know that I had a plan if he was down for some sneaking.

On the night of the plan, he came to the house excited. I let him in through the side door and into the basement. My cousin was staying over this night and she was sleeping in the living room, so she heard the side door open. She came down to see what was going on, and I begged her not to say anything. She said okay, told me to be careful, and went upstairs to go back to sleep. As we got started, we jumped from first base straight to fourth in a matter of seconds. Before fourth base was started I asked him if he had protection, and he pulled it out and said yes. Our fourth base session started behind me, so I didn't see him apply the protection, but I did hear him open the wrapper. After about 10 minutes into home base, I realized I did not feel the protection I thought he applied. I told him to stop. He ignored me and kept going. I said it again, and when he didn't stop, I had to actually get up from where I was. When I got up and turned around to look, there was no protection. I told him to get out. He got mad and grabbed his stuff and left. As soon as he left, I changed his number in my phone to "DO NOT ANSWER."

I saw that phrase come across my phone every hour of every day for the next week. I never answered for him. Every time he would text me to plead with me, and ask what he did wrong, I would say, "you know what you did" and leave it at that. That was not enough for him. He started threatening to show up at the house and tell my aunty everything. I was so scared that I actually took his call after that. He begged and pleaded with me to let him come over again and I told him no.

I guess he didn't want to take no for an answer, so he turned into a monster. He started editing the photos I sent him with words written across saying "This girl has HIV/AIDS!!! Don't mess with her." He sent that to me one day. He told me he was sending this to all the guys on the block. He told me the whole eastside of Detroit would know where I lived and how nasty I was. It was traumatizing to say the least. I didn't know who to talk to about this in the moment. I wanted to tell my aunty, but I knew she would kill me. I blocked him out of my phone, but by that time it was too late. He had already gotten my aunty's number from the voicemail on my phone, which was originally her phone and number. That night he called my aunty and told her everything.

As anyone could imagine, once my aunty answered the phone and talked to this guy she was shocked, angry, and ready for war. He certainly embellished the story and incorporated lies within his truth of knowing where we lived and being in the house before. He even told her his real age. To my surprise, he was actually in his late twenties from what he told my aunty. Due to him being honest about his age, he lied to her and said that he never had sex with me. He told her I only performed third base for him. However, third base was never in any of our interactions. She didn't even give me a chance to explain before she started giving me the beat down of my life. I couldn't even fight her back because I very much well deserved it. She made me pack all of my things in trash bags while she beat me up. She called and told everybody in the car on the way to dropping me off to my mama's house.

He didn't stop with that one call. He kept calling my aunty with more lies once he realized she was going to hurt me for everything he told her. He wanted me to feel whatever it was he felt when I decided to block him and never deal with him again. He even lied about my cousin who was there that night saying she was involved as well. After so many calls, he began harassing my aunty, and sending her all the photos I ever sent him. It was a disaster.

At my mama's house I had to come clean about everything. I told everything that happened to everyone who came over and asked questions. I even told my mama and aunties how he sent the

HIV/AIDS photos to me saying this is what I had as a result of sleeping with him. One of my aunties decided it was a good idea to take me to the hospital to get checked and treated for every sexually transmitted disease (STD) he said I had. I was scared because I remembered feeling unprotected that night of the act.

When we went to the hospital the nurses had so many questions, and I had little to no answers to give them. They performed a rape kit after I explained the full story of how I ended up in this position. They also ran tests for diseases and told me everything came back negative. However, since the incident was recent, they treated me for every STD I could have possibly been exposed to. They mentioned some of the diseases could take time to show up, so they wanted to prevent it from the start. They gave me injections in my arms that burned for syphilis and gonorrhea prevention. They gave me pills to take for chlamydia prevention. Then they sent me home with two bottles worth of pills to take for HIV/AIDS prevention over the course of 4 weeks. I had to take 4 pills a day for 4 weeks straight. I felt devastated.

The first week of taking all those pills was the worst I ever felt in my life. I was regurgitating every day. I couldn't keep heavy food down for the whole 4 weeks I had to take those pills. The only things I remember eating during that time were peanut butter and jelly sandwiches and crackers here and there. I lost so much weight that summer. Although I was thankful to be STD free, my experience was miserable. It was absolutely the worst summer of my life.

I eventually had to go to the police station and file a restraining order against the guy. The issue with that was I didn't even know his last name. The detective looked at me and asked me if I knew the full name of the guy. Once I told him no, he shook his head at me. The fact that I was so willing to give my body away to a guy that I barely knew was mind boggling for him. For me, that is when I knew for sure that I had a problem. My promiscuous acts not only led me to a stalker that I barely knew, but it sent me down a path of fear for my health and having to get my whole family involved in my drama. I was put out of my aunty's house and left without a job as well. Having sex frequently to fill the voids in my heart was a blind remedy that didn't work. However, that fact didn't stop me from trying to make it work.

Once school started back, I changed my behavior drastically. I went back to being the straight A student who danced all the time. I tried my best to shut down the longings to be touched I had within me. No matter how hard I tried, my body still wanted the fix. In an attempt to be more civilized with my passions, I got into a relationship. For my last two years of high school I had a boyfriend who was indeed willing to fulfill whatever cravings I had. However, I had a lot of personal issues that came with those cravings. I realized that I was having sex to cover pain in my life. Whenever I wanted to feel a different energy outside of my current circumstances, I used sex to get there. My boyfriend couldn't fix those issues. I made yet another mistake of trying to make him my fixer. That relationship eventually went south, and my promiscuity struggle reappeared in my last year of college.

How This Worked For Me

"It is God's will that you should be sanctified: that you should avoid sexual immorality; that each of you should learn to control your own body in a way that is holy and honorable, not in passionate lust like the pagans, who do not know God."

1 Thessalonians 4:3-5 (NIV)

My explanation for this chapter is something I know won't be for everybody. Sexual purity is such an unpopular topic in today's society, but it was the only thing that rescued me from a life of self-destruction. The night I was exposed in my activities, I prayed to God that if He would rescue me from that situation, then I would never have sex before marriage again. He and I both knew that was a lie, but I thought maybe my experience was punishment for not listening when my daddy said waiting until marriage was the Godly thing to do. Trying to stop sex cold turkey without the understanding of sexual purity only led to masturbation and pornography addiction many times in my life. There was something I was missing in the call to holiness.

I couldn't grasp the idea of holiness because my views on sex were so blurred and broken. I was broken. I was a young girl with curves that men saw and lusted after. The attention given to me because of how I looked, excited me. The desires brewing deep within me only added fuel to that fire. I knew what I was doing was wrong. Somehow, I didn't seem to care until it shook my whole world up. My dysfunctional intimacy with men was set up to fail from the start. That start happened in my *Crummy Secrets* chapter. From then on, I never knew or understood my worth.

I mentioned the root of where lust stemmed from in my life in *Crummy Secrets*. The only way planted seeds grow roots is through watering those seeds. I watered lust by my curiosity of what it could fulfill in me. The voids that I developed in my heart from my parental issues, feelings of abandonment, neglect and being misunderstood were crying out to be filled. I tried filling those voids with sex. For a while it worked. So I thought. But it left me empty inside, because that particular cure was never enough. Once lust begins to grow it wants more and more, and if you feed that more than you feed your relationship with God, it can consume you.

My lust and desires for love drove me to unfathomable measures of trying to satisfy my cravings. In the midst of me doing everything I was doing, God protected me from diseases, unplanned pregnancies, kidnap, sex trafficking and so much more. I didn't ask for that protection, but He did it for me anyway. I needed to learn a lesson that I couldn't pinpoint in those moments. It was the lesson of holiness and purity. These lessons were taught to me through growing in my relationship with God.

For me, fulfilling my lustful desires showed evidence in my lack of intimacy with God. When you really begin to spend time with God and allow His love and presence to consume your life, you won't have room in your heart for desires that did not come from Him. Due to us living a human experience on earth, it is impossible to ignore the physical yearnings we have in our bodies. That is why self-control is such an important fruit of the Spirit to obtain as we try to know God.

Intimacy with God is knowing God. The more you know about Him, the more you love Him. The more you love Him, the more you want His will for your life and not your own. Desiring His will for your life helps you see the importance of purity and holiness. It preserves your integrity to yourself and God's people. These truths helped me avoid so many more mistakes I could have made when I finally studied it. I hate that I had to go through that. I hate that I still didn't learn my lesson for years after that. Once I finally understood it, I could see how God could use even my very mistakes for growth in my life. I am grateful that I lived to share my testimony.

Chapter Six

Disappointment Works

Ever since I was 15 years old, I knew exactly what I wanted to do in life. That desire still has not changed to this very day. My dream is to become one of the world's greatest talk show hosts. It started in middle school when I would talk to friends who often expressed to me their life situations freely without any borders in their vulnerability. By the time high school came around, I was still that "go to" person for many people who wanted or needed to talk. I would always feel like a counselor or therapist in some situations.

Although my first goal in life was to dance background for Ciara, I knew I had another gift to serve others, and help them figure out life in most circumstances. Why I thought I could do that as a teenager, I don't know, but I believe God put that desire in me. I remember telling my mama one day that I wanted to be a therapist. She said, "Okay, that's good."

Shortly after that Mama would be watching *The Tyra Banks Show* every day when I came home from school. The show caught my attention, so I started watching too. I was so intrigued and inspired I loved every aspect of her show. They talked about everything! There was no topic off limits. Tyra would literally roll on the floor laughing at her guests if they said something funny. Not only that, she stuck to her first love, which is all things modeling and beauty and incorporated that in almost all of her shows. I eventually said to myself, "I want to do that!"

With my vivacious personality, and constantly being reprimanded for talking too much in class, I knew I couldn't be contained in an office. When I figured it all out, I went to my mama and said, "Mama, I have decided, if I do any kind of therapy, I want it to be on TV! People can come sit on my couch and talk to me live! I'm going to be a talk show host!" She said, "That's good Porchia! You do like to talk a lot. So that's better for you. You can do it!" I took that and ran with it. It was the only confirmation I have ever needed to this day.

While attending Detroit School of Arts (DSA) for high school, I became a dance major. It was my goal to stay true to my first love just like Tyra did in her show. I remember telling people what I wanted to do after high school and college, and people would ask me, "so why are you a dance major?" That question often made me laugh, but I can understand the confusion.

DSA is an outstanding performing arts school. We didn't have sports at our school because we put so much focus into our talents and artistic gifts. Our classes pertaining to our major was half or even sometimes the majority of our day. Due to my goals in life, people thought I should have majored in the Radio/TV program. Since I knew that would be my focus in college, I would tell people that I'm going to incorporate dance into my talk show one day.

When high school graduation came around, I had it all mapped out. I was going to go to Los Angeles, CA, and getting a bachelor's degree in the School of Journalism at University of Southern California (USC). I figured since I would already be in L.A., my career would take off from there. It wasn't until I received that rejection letter from USC that my goals and plans had to change. At the time, USC required a 3.7 GPA and a 32 for an ACT score. I however only had a 3.4 GPA and a 19 for an ACT score. I felt like they could have made an exception for me, and I took the rejection personally.

I figured that USC just didn't want some little black girl from Detroit coming to their school and making it "ghetto." I know that is not true, however, I did not take rejection well at that time. I simply did not meet the requirements. But I didn't let that stop my collegiate journey to be educated in the career I wanted. I knew that I would take my talents and intellect to a school where they would accept me with open arms. I decided that I would attend a historically black college or university (HBCU).

I was so very fortunate to be accepted by and attend the illustrious Tennessee State University (TSU), which we know as the Land of Golden Sunshine. This was very exciting to me because they were the first school to accept me out of the 3 HBCUs I applied to. Although I was accepted by the others as well, I knew it was a go with TSU after doing my research on the school. I found that they had an amazing Mass Communications program that I imagined myself being a part of before even arriving. The motto for TSU is "Think. Work. Serve." and that was all I had planned to do with my life.

I also knew that Oprah Winfrey attended TSU when she was in college, and I decided to follow her journey to success. Although I was majorly inspired by Tyra and her show, I found out that Oprah excelled in this career more than anyone. If I wanted to be the best in this business, then I had to follow the blueprint of the greatest talk show host of all time.

Since TSU is a place where we "enter to learn and go forth to serve," I didn't want to waste any time. My plans were to learn everything I possibly could while trying my best to stay away from distractions. In that case, I could leave there with enough knowledge to work and serve in my career of choice. Although I was a first-generation college student for my immediate family, I witnessed my cousin Diamond go to college 2 years before me, and she completed her undergraduate studies in 3 years. I wanted that for me too. I went into college knowing that I would graduate in 3 years instead of 4. I was on a mission. I had my mind set on dominating the Mass Communications programs, all while doing whatever I could to follow and educate myself in the journey of Oprah Winfrey.

My first step on the campus of TSU took my breath away. I started school in the fall semester of the year 2012. The campus was huge and beautiful to say the least. All I saw were people laughing, smiling, talking, dancing and eating everywhere. This consistent joy and liveliness happened every single day. I loved the students. I liked most of the faculty. I wasn't, however, too fond of the long financial aid lines, or the fact that I had all of my classes purged at least twice while attending. Most of the dorm and campus apartment situations were okay enough to say I had the experience.

My favorite day of the week was "fried chicken Wednesday" because that was my favorite food at the time. My friends and I would enjoy that day in the cafeteria every week; even when we didn't have meal plans purchased on our ID card. Between that and the Chik-Fil-A on campus, I gained a "freshman 30" as opposed to the usual "freshman 15," and those pounds stuck with me until I graduated. Walking the campus of TSU looked like walking around at a festival full of young Black Excellence. This was an ongoing festival for the next few years to come.

I pursued my Bachelor of Arts degree in Mass Communications with an emphasis in Media Leadership and Performance.

Fortunately for me, that track was created during my second semester at TSU. I originally had an emphasis in journalism, but I wanted to expand my horizon. I got involved in all realms of media including hosting, news, radio, acting, video production, and TV programing. For the Media Leadership and Performance track, I needed 120 credits to graduate. I took 15 credits per semester, and due to me maintaining a 3.4 grade point average, I was awarded the opportunity to take a free Maymester course each year.

Maymester is a short semester that occurs in the month of May and is available at no cost for students with a 3.0 grade point average or higher. If a student were to achieve a B or higher in their Maymester course, then they were awarded a free summer semester course as well. I took full advantage of those opportunities because I was determined to graduate early. As long as I graduated by the end of 2015, then my 3 year mission would be complete. By the time my junior year came to an end, I had 107 credits. Although I only needed 13 more to graduate with, I was scheduled for 15 the upcoming Fall semester.

I also achieved my goals of dominating in my field of studies. I made As in 95% of my major's courses. By my sophomore year, I had been a host and producer of a few radio shows. I became Operations Manager of WTST The Blaze radio station. I was one of the appointed news anchors and reporters for TSU TV News. And I also became the general manager of the TSU TV 98, even though I only managed my own shows during my time in leadership. I loved my work and was very proud of the things I had accomplished in such a short amount of time. However, I didn't stop there.

During the course of my attendance, I made it my business to get acquainted with the majority of the students on campus. Since

I had been a social butterfly all of my life, I began to engage with so many different people from all walks of life, and that made my TSU life way more exciting. I joined a host of organizations during my undergraduate studies. I was inducted into the Phi Eta Sigma Honors society where I met a few friends my freshman year. I became a member of HIP'Notyze Dance Troupe where I met the majority of my friends who are still friends to this day. Although I only performed with our organization a few times, it kept my passion for dance ignited throughout college. I was also inducted into the National Association of Colored Women's Clubs (NACWC), the Women of Empowerment chapter. This organization gave me so much knowledge on the prominence of being a black woman in America. Last but not least, I pledged Delta Sigma Theta Sorority Incorporated, the Alpha Chi chapter. Although I am no longer a part of the sorority, I gained 58 sisters who I love and cherish more than words can describe. Because of them, my last few semesters at TSU were a blast!

The joys and treasures of the HBCU experience took over my whole existence. The rich history and spirit of excellence was prevalent. I was learning so many things about black culture that I didn't know outside of the city I grew up in. I cherished being a part of something so significant to my legacy as a black individual in America. I was enjoying this life to the fullest! I loved TSU, the students, and my department of studies so much that I chose to go deeper in my involvement with the university.

I decided to become a campus queen and join the Royal Court. I always admired the royal court for their presence on campus, and I knew that if I would do anything in the Student Government Association (SGA), then it would be in that area. Being a member of the Royal Court meant being the face of the university in your specific classification. You are either a Miss/Mister of your particular class, or the ultimate reign of Miss/Mister TSU. When I decided to join the Royal Court, I was a sophomore, so I had to run for the title of Miss Junior.

My Miss Junior campaign was pretty cute. The theme was the Miss Carter Show, playing off of Beyonce's recent tour that year, with inclusion of my last name. I actually wore a leotard and crown for my photo shoot to recreate the cover art of the actual tour. I was told it wasn't the "queenliest" idea, but I still pulled it off. During my events, I owned the "Heyyyyy Miss Carter" call and response just like Beyonce as well. I was surprised at all the love and support I received. By the end of Student Election Commission (SEC) week, I felt like I had accomplished a successful campaign. I assumed my class felt the same because I won and was crowned Miss Junior of Tennessee State University for the 2014-2015 academic school year.

Becoming a campus queen was way more work than I thought. I was being taught another level of etiquette. If I thought I was lady-like before, then queen days made me think again. I had to be presentable at times. I couldn't go to class with a regular t-shirt and jogging pants on, I had to wear blouses with skirts or dresses for the most part. I wore a crown and sash every week. We had to be present in the stands for every football game during the entire season. We got the opportunity to go to some of the away games too.

My favorite away game that year was the Southern Heritage Classic, where we played against Jackson State University in Memphis, TN. We started out the day in pep rallies and parades where we rode on the back of convertibles and wave to the TSU alumni and current students who came for the Classic. I loved every second of us being recognized on the field for big games. We always did our regular chants and dances with the band as they played in the stands, but this day they were going harder than ever, and

I believe this is the weekend they started playing Melodies from Heaven by Kirk Franklin. The Aristocrat of Bands is literally the best band in the land. To top things off for the Classic, we won the game! Then after our win, they displayed fireworks over the field as we sang our TSU theme song.

Although my appearance was changing drastically, and I was having a ball as a queen with all the glamour and recognition, my character wasn't keeping up with the changes. I still wanted to have fun. During my junior year I was the queen of my class and also a cohabitant of the "*Delta House*." The *Delta House* was the campus apartment where me and 3 of my line sisters decided to be roommates. There was no other apartment on campus filled with only Deltas, so our apartment became the "Turnt House" as well. Turnt is an expression of liveliness, excitement, fun, and the majority of the time, drunkenness. We had plenty of crazy parties ("sets" in TSU language).

We would get in trouble for some of the parties because half of the campus queens were Deltas and two of them were my roommates. Britney, my next-door roommate was Miss Collegiate 100. Shanyn, who was in the room next to Britney, was actually Miss Senior. Although she wasn't our roommate, the current Miss TSU that year was our line sister Sam.

As a campus queen, my *turnt* life at the *Delta House* was probably unacceptable. However, we did incorporate prayer nights for our weekday routine whenever we wanted to pray over test, grades, tuition costs and everything else we were facing during that time. People came to pray with us during the week. Then we showed them a good time on the weekends. It worked for us. It is safe to say that I was the most *turnt* member of the *Delta House*, which was bad, because I was the youngest campus queen in the house. It wasn't even legal for me to be drinking the way that I was. I ended up turning 21 the second semester of my junior year and the legal aspect of my behavior changed.

Even in my "turnt life" I was still able to host events for students and gave away a book scholarship during my term as Miss Junior. My popularity had grown so much between the Mass Comm department, my various organization participation, My Royal Court life, and the "turnt life." It was almost as if I began to feel invincible at TSU. When the time came up for new SGA role submissions, I was approached with the idea to run for the biggest queen opportunity on campus, MISS TSU! I was slightly hesitant at first because the term to serve as queen would extend my stay to a complete 4 years rather than the 3 years I had planned.

On the other hand, I knew I was popular. I was already a campus queen, so I had the experience under my belt. I had ideas for more programs and things I could do for the school. I loved everything about TSU, including the learning and growth I had been experiencing. Plus, I was willing to do anything required of me to make my campus proud. When I came to the final decision, it was a no-brainer. I believed that if I could serve as Miss TSU, then the exposure from being the queen of a whole school would propel me into my dreams, and I would accelerate faster than usual on my journey. So, I entered myself in the running for the ultimate queen position, Miss TSU.

My decision to run was made so last minute that I didn't have time to fully prepare for the campaign. However, I wanted to win this opportunity so bad that I prayed to God every single day about it. I believed in my heart that this was something God wanted me to do because things literally started coming together for me. Money for the campaign was coming out of nowhere. I was able to schedule photo shoots, print flyers, plan event reservations, and order t-shirts done in a short time period.

My campaign theme for Miss TSU was simply, PORCHIA. The tag line was, The Ultimate Vehicle to Drive You to a New TSU. This was a play off me being named after the car Porsche. I used the first few seconds of T-Wayne's song Nasty Freestyle as my theme song during the whole campaign and the camps loved it. I played it at all of my events, and I danced to it on two occasions during my SEC week performances.

Although I had a sense of invincibility and depended strongly on my popularity, I was still nervous during SEC week. This campaign was way different than my Miss Junior campaign. I had to participate in debates, a pageant, and frequent speeches and still be fully present at every single event I had. I was no longer trying to just appease a particular classification; I was now trying to win the validation of the whole school.

I was rehearsing every night for the pageant. I was showing up to every dorm to talk to students and pass out flyers. I was making consistent appearances in the student center, cafeteria and even showing up to classrooms to promote at one point. This SEC week took so much out of me. I felt like I had stripped myself naked and put myself out on display for the whole campus to pick apart and judge every single flaw I had.

That is exactly what they did too. People started digging up dirt and creating rumors and dragging my name through the mud in order to make my opponent look better than me. Not only that, due to my current place of residents and the lifestyle I lived after I took my crown off, I was labelled as the "Turnt Queen." Some of the people who gave me that label told me I was way too "Turnt" to be Miss TSU and that I should just give up.

I didn't let any of that discourage me. I knew I still had a chance. I just started showing up more and giving more of myself. I even did an amazing job in the pageant with my speech, and dance performance. Plus, my daddy came to walk me down the aisle of my formal wear portion of the pageant. All of my prayers had been answered concerning this endeavor, so I knew it was mine to have.

On the day of the announcement, I walked in with my head held high. I actually sat next to my opponent Tyra in the Forum before we prepared to go outside to hear the results. Tyra said something so profound that I would always remember. She said, "if either of us lose we have to know that this too shall pass." I understood what she said in that moment, but I just knew that I wouldn't have to think on those words for me. Then we went outside for the results.

The announcements were set up to announce the exact number of votes for each person in the running. When they announced the winner for Miss TSU, they always announced the person with the least votes first. So, when they called my name first, I was so confused. I just knew that they had it all wrong. I just knew they were announcing my votes out of order. I knew that once they said the number of votes for Tyra, that it would be a lower number than mine. But it wasn't.

When I didn't hear a lower number of votes, it was as if the whole world stopped spinning for me and me only. I was in a daze. I'm sure everyone around me was jumping around for joy in celebration of all the wins announced, but for me, everything was frozen. I couldn't hear anything but my heartbeat. The weight of disappointment had consumed me. I couldn't return to the *Delta House* that day because I knew so many students who had worked on my campaign were there waiting for me to come back with good news. So, I went to my line sister Tameria's apartment. She gave me her bed for the night.

The next day, Tameria woke me up and said let's go for a ride. I was so disappointed and distraught that I couldn't even function. She took me to Centennial Park and told me to let it all out. That moment in her car was my first time letting out a cry. I cried, I screamed, and I talked about how I couldn't believe I lost. It was the biggest loss I ever had in my life that I put myself out there for.

I cried because I started to believe what people were saying about me was true. I also felt low because I was a current queen and the Delta who lost Miss TSU. I felt like I had let my sorority down as well as all the wonderful students who believed in me. I was disappointed in myself for thinking I had what it took to be Miss TSU. I was disappointed in the way I let people talk about me without clapping back at them because I just knew I would win. I was disappointed because so many people had given funds to help this campaign that failed.

I was also very disappointed in God because I thought this was something that He okayed me to do. The plan I created to use that platform to propel me forward in my dreams had crumbled. In that moment, I remembered what it is that I actually wanted to do, and that's when Tyra's words came back to me. "This too shall pass."

How This Worked For Me

"In their hearts humans plan their course, but the Lord establishes their steps."

Proverbs 16:9 (ESV)

My experience as campus queen had already run its course. Everything I needed and wanted out of that experience; I had received.

It was the pride in me that made me feel like I could go to the next level and dominate it. My plans to use the Miss TSU platform to climb to my next level was only distracting me from my actual goals. I never even unpacked what it was I thought having that position was supposed to do for my career. I just wanted it so bad because popularity on that level fed my prideful desires for potential fame. I had to remember what it was I was trying to do with my life, and why. Although I was sold on my plan being a good thing for me, good distractions are still distractions.

Once I shook off the disappointment of losing that title, I got back into action. I refocused and went back to working on the reason why I had gone to TSU in the first place. That summer I had more time on my hands to do everything I needed to do in preparation for my departure. I landed a production assistant internship at News Channel 5 in Nashville, TN. This was the same news station where Oprah began her journalism career. I learned all of the procedures for how a news station operates. I assisted in the on-air production of morning talk shows and nightly news. I took everything I learned and applied it to my own projects when I returned to school.

In my last semester of college, I created my own talk show titled *The Porchia Carter Show*. I talked about love, beauty, health, purpose, and dream chasing on my show. I wanted to create something inspiring, motivating, and meaningful for my audience, and I did just that. I was the producer, the writer, the segment producer, director, host and editor of my show. I mainly had help on set when it was actually time to record my shows.

One of my favorite professors, Mrs. Morris helped with audio while friends and students helped with stage managing and arranging guests. I was able to employ students who needed extra credit in my department, and our professors allowed them to work on my show to achieve it. Due to me doing all those things, I gained so much knowledge in the area of talk show production. This was something I would not have had the time for had I won Miss TSU.

I was also able to use my show title to host seminars, book signings, and talent showcases which the students loved. I didn't miss out on doing any of the programs and events I actually wanted to do. The greatest win of all was that I still graduated in 3 years as originally planned. In December of 2015, I walked across the stage with my Bachelor of Arts degree in Mass Communications; a semester earlier than I was supposed to. That would not have been the case if I was still a campus queen. Graduating early was one of my biggest goals and I accomplished it. This opened my eyes to the fact that most disappointments are actually blessings in disguise.

Chapter Seven

Ending Relationships Work

During the development of my life, I have found that relationships are important. I also realize how much I cherish the relationships in my life because of how important they are. We need people in our lives because that's how God's will is accomplished; through people. God also blesses us with different relationships to help us along in our life's journey. Some of those relationships are family, friends, associates, business partners, neighbors, and romantic relationships. No matter what kind of relationship I have built with someone in my life, I never expect, want, or intend for them to end when they do. This has caused me many tears, heartache, and confusion dealing with the area of forgiveness.

I'm usually not the type to cut people off and disregard them like they're nothing after a relationship comes to an unexpected end. I have always needed clarity or "closure" in order to make the break-up from meaningful relationships official. If the person did something wrong, hurtful or disrespectful, it's a lot easier to cut them off rather than when you just don't know or don't understand why it's ending. I have found myself in quite a few unexpected endings that left me feeling broken. I had a friend who stopped being my friend because I was too "clingy." I also had a friend who stopped talking to me because I was not meeting their unspoken expectations in our friendship. I don't know how that made sense to them, but it left me confused, hurt, and angry before eventually deciding I was done with them, too.

Building meaningful and healthy relationships of all kinds takes work, communication, and authenticity. When those aspects are lacking, confusion is then stirred up. Most of my issues in this area have come from romantic relationships. Too many times I have dealt with young men putting in the work to get to know my body rather than me. That has led to communication issues, because complaining and arguing were the results of no real work being done. Once chaos sets in, authenticity is foggy because you'll never see the genuine parts of people if all you do is dispute with them. In my current 26 years of life, I have only had 3 "real boyfriends." All of these relationships happened before age 22, and I'm so grateful for growth. I have spent these last 4 years of singleness reflecting on all the things that went wrong in my past relationships, and I'd like to share one of my personal romantic relationship stories with you. We will call this guy "Dude."

Dude and I met during my junior year of college. I was strolling with my line sisters at a nightclub when I locked eyes with a guy who was eagerly staring at me. When we were done, he came up to me asking me how I was doing with the biggest grin I had ever seen on a man. Our conversation was short because I wasn't trying to entertain him. When we went back to the apartment that night, my line sister asked if I knew who the guy was that came up to me and I told her no. She let me know that it was Dude, a party promoter, and he told her, "I want your Deuce (which is my line number)." I laughed it off because at the time, I wasn't interested. I had other stuff going on that I was focused on.

Shortly after that initial meeting, Dude came over to one of our *Delta House* sets (kick back/party). I couldn't help but notice him trying to attract my attention the whole night, and I eventually gave in and had a conversation with him which stirred up a whole lot of jokes, laughs, and excitement. The next thing I knew, he was still there after most people had left, and we were up talking until the sun came up. This exact situation happened for the next few nights to follow. By this time the fall semester had ended, so our sets went from Thursday through Saturday, to Monday through Saturday. There were fewer people on campus at the time because most students had gone home for winter break already. That didn't stop the few of us who hung on campus from coming over every night. Dude wouldn't hesitate to show up consistently with the turn up (beer/liquor) making sure he contributed to our nightly excitement. I appreciated the fact that he never showed up empty handed. It made me feel like he really cared.

Dude popped up to our apartment most nights. He became the life of the party for me because the time we spent together made me think he was so cool. He gave me so much attention. We talked on the phone every day whenever he wasn't at my apartment about almost everything under the sun. He told me about his life and his journey with being in college. He said he was in a fraternity and had pledged to that fraternity 3 years before I pledged mine. He mentioned that he was 25 years old, and still in undergrad because he took some time off after he lost one of his closest friends.

That made sense to me inquiring why he was still on campus if he pledged his fraternity his junior year of college. I was only 20 when we met, but I didn't think anything of our age difference. I was open with him and he was open with me. The best part was he never mentioned the topic of sex in any of our conversations, so for me, he became the first person ever to not pursue me for my body or beautiful face. We were actually getting to know each other for real.

Right before I made it home for Christmas, my grandpa passed away, and it shook me to my core. This was my first time ever losing anyone in my family on my maternal side. I left Nashville and went home to Detroit the next day to be with my family to help plan for everything. I remember not going to sleep the night before the funeral, and Dude was in constant communication with me through texts. I believe we talked on the phone for a little while too. Talking to him while I prepared the slide show of my grandpa's photos helped me so much and made me appreciate his conversation tremendously.

After the funeral, I heard that the city of Nashville was dropping a guitar on New Year's night. My grandpa was well known for playing the guitar, and he played for us whenever he had the chance. It was one of my favorite memories of him, so I decided I would go back to Nashville New Year's night with my uncle and aunt who lived there and had driven up for the funeral.

By the time I returned to Nashville I had only an hour to get myself ready to go downtown. I did my make-up, and dressed quickly, and had enough time to pregame with my friends before we left out. By then I was super tipsy, running through the streets of downtown Nashville with heels on, trying to make it to see this guitar drop at midnight. I ran into people and I stumbled upon strollers and everything else that was in my way. I felt like I was almost there, but as I stumbled closer, the countdown for the new year had already started. By the time everyone started shouting Happy New Year, I realized I had missed it. The guitar dropped and so did my heart for not being there to see it.

I was disappointed and ready to go back to my apartment. When we arrived back at the *Delta House*, a few people had already started to gather for a small afterparty to bring in the year. I drank as much as I could before heading to bed because I was still disappointed with my night. On my way to bed, Dude showed up. We were both drunk, so I knew no decent conversations were about to take place that night.

However, we were both excited to see each other. He came into my room, picked me up and he hugged me extremely tight. I was so vulnerable at the time, but I felt so safe in his arms. I immediately started crying my eyes out. I told him how I could not believe my grandpa had died. I told him that I felt like a failure for missing the guitar drop. I cried about all the grief and pain I was feeling in that moment. After I cried it all out, he wiped my tears, and told me everything was going to be okay. Then he kissed me. That kiss led to a fourth base encounter that changed my world.

I had no idea that I could be addicted to someone the way I was with him. What was once progressing into a healthy friendship filled with great conversation, eventually turned into a whirlpool of "relations." The consistent, long, intriguing conversations were replaced with sexual nightcaps. Whenever we did talk, the conversations were still intriguing, just not as long as they used to be. I didn't know what happened, or how it happened so fast, but for some reason I was okay with it.

It was almost as if his sex fixed my grief and everything else I was going through during those times in my life. It wasn't until a few months in, when I decided that I wanted more from him than that. I began asking the question, "what are we?" He never gave me a straight answer. He was at my apartment nearly every day talking, eating and entertaining our friends, while in my bed practically every night, so I felt like we should progress to actually being a couple. He didn't want a title to complicate what we had going on, so that led to a few disagreements.

People around campus started to notice how close he and I were growing, so that brought another wave of attention and unwanted conversations my way. I remember going to meet with a beautiful young lady who called me over to give me the scoop on Dude. She told me that whatever he mentioned about his life was a lie. She explained that she found his driver's license one day, and it read a birth year that didn't match the age he told her he was. She said he also wasn't in school anymore, neither did he have a real job. He was a 27-year-old fulltime party promoter. He only tells younger girls that he's 25 and still in school, so that could give him a reason to still be on campus scouting us out. Of course, she had been with him before, but he was at her house "just to sleep" before coming to my apartment for the night. That is why she thought I should know.

That was a lot of information for me to process. I thanked her for her information, and immediately went to him with what she said. He denied every single detail of her facts except the fact that he went there a few nights prior to sleep. I was so confused. He was so smooth, devious, and charming that I believed his words. He had a way of transitioning himself from topics of discussion and redirecting them to focus on me. (If that just made any sense to you, then you've been there before for sure!) He began talking to me as if he wanted to finally be with me. Once he told me that he didn't want to lose me, that was it for me, I was all in again. I threw away every thought of doubt I had about him after a soothing conversation and sensual nightcap.

After a while I realized that he was no longer talking as if us being together was our next step. We were back to our regularly scheduled program. He was saying we didn't need a title with his mouth, but he was acting like my boyfriend with everything else. Plus, I had given this man full access to me at any given time of the day or night, and all the "boyfriend privileges" he subconsciously asked for. Although he was saying he wasn't my boyfriend, I took it upon myself to start treating him as such. I claimed him to be mine in my head.

One night, before leaving the club where he was working, I tried to take a picture with him even though I knew it was something he didn't like. We had been doing our thing with each other for the past 6 months, so I didn't think a photo was too much to ask. This was my first time asking for a photo in public, so I guess that turned him off. Although he eventually took the picture with me, he still had an attitude which he displayed toward me. I didn't feel like arguing because I was way too "turnt" at the time, but I did display a little push back. I ended our conversation letting him know that I would see him at my place shortly. I knew our routine night cap would solve anything like it always did.

After hours of waiting for him, he still hadn't come knocking at my door like I expected even though I called him and he said he was coming over. Frustrated and angry, I left my apartment around 3 AM to hunt for him. When I went to the campus apartment where he had said he was playing games with a friend, Dude wasn't there. When I demanded to see him, Guy responded, "What? Dude ain't been here all night!" I said, "Oh for real?" And at that point it was on.

I stormed away from those apartments and went back to mine, heated and ready for war. I instantly figured he must be with another girl. I kept replaying all of Dude's lies in my head. I kept telling myself how I can't believe I was sitting here letting myself get played by a "bum nigga!" I felt like if he was in my bed almost every night and talking to me almost every day, then he was mine! And I refused to be cheated on. I know we didn't have a title, but he belonged to me and he wasn't allowed to be with anyone else. He especially couldn't be with another girl while we were supposed to be having our routine nightcap.

I borrowed my roommate's car and drove to the house he said he had been house sitting for a family member. I pulled up and saw his car parked in the front, and another car in the driveway. I looked inside of the other car for any evidence and saw a pair of women's gym shoes in the back seat. I knew this car had to belong to another woman. Outraged and jealous, I banged on his doors and windows, screaming and yelling for him to come outside and face me. When I got tired of waiting for him to come out, I took the keys that were in my hand, and decided to carve a message for him along the whole side of his dearly beloved car. I wrote, "DON'T PLAY WITH ME!!" in all caps as big as I could fit it. Then I drove back to my own apartment.

Immediately afterwards, he was blowing my phone up and we yelled and screamed at each other once I finally answered. He thought I was crazy for ruining his car, and I felt angry because he had lied to me. For the next few days, he threatened to press charges against me for vandalism and about a week later I decided to just pay him the $250 he said it would cost to fix the damages so that he would leave me alone.

When he came to pick up the money, he mentioned that he thought I was crazy for what I did, and he was extremely angry at me. But some part of him realized what he would be losing by losing me. He said my actions woke him up and made him realize how much I meant to him. I could not believe what he was saying. I was highly confused. I thought that my acting out ended whatever it is that we had for good. But he looked at me and assured me that he just needed some space and time. I was still upset and over him, so I let his words go in one ear and out the other.

However, due to the fact that I had created a really strong soul tie with Dude, I was craving him greatly. I decided to start messing around with other guys as a means to the phrase, "get over your old man by getting under a new one." That was so stupid of me. It didn't work out. While I was doing that, I would have sporadic conversations with Dude that would all lead to arguments because I still had so many unanswered questions as to why he thought he could play with me. After having other relations and realizing that they were in no comparison to the relations I had with Dude, I felt frustrated. I felt like I needed something or someone to replace that space in my heart and body that he had once occupied. In my frustration, I decided to start back having sex with Dude, while dating other guys at the same time.

One day Dude came over to our planned nightcap super drunk. He was very belligerent, angry, and passionate all at the same time. We couldn't even have a decent conversation. There was only yelling and screaming going on to the point of us almost physically fighting. I couldn't understand what was wrong with him, but I thought back to all the times he came over drunk to the *Delta House* when I stayed there. I realized I had ignored the signs that some conversations triggered anger during his intoxication.

I was so mad at his current state that I asked him to leave. On his way out he said some really degrading things to me, and that was it for me. I went in. I don't know what all I said, but I know by the time I was done, his face was crushed. I used my mouth to cut him deep. Then I topped it off with, "I don't need you, I'm messing with so and so anyway! And he knows exactly how to treat me!" That brought him to his knees. He literally pinned me down and asked me if I was giving what was his to another man. I told him yes because I wasn't his. He dang near cried. He told me

I needed to cut off the other man ASAP. I said, "I'm not cutting nobody off for you. You ain't my man!" He said okay and he left.

That argument that night was a lot and should have been the last straw with Dude. However, it sparked him to commit to our relationship. A few days later he asked if we could talk. I agreed and let him come over and he apologized for his actions sincerely. Then he hit me with that "I don't want to lose you" game again. He made it sound so sweet, that I was open and ready to hear more. He said that he wanted to be with me, but his only requirement was that I had to cut off the other guy I started talking to. I said okay and deleted his number right then and there. Then he said with his mouth that from that day forth, I was officially his girlfriend. I was so excited as if I had forgotten about all the lies, the constant reg flags and everything else I had been through with him for the past 7 months or so. Before I could even think about all those things, we had already sealed our relationship with a nightcap. From that point on, I was all in.

This newfound relationship between us was an amazingly blissful fresh start. Dude totally changed in the best possible way. He showed me love continuously all day every day. He would make sure things I needed were taken care of. He was extremely sweet to me and would say some of the most romantic things ever. He upped his joke game to keep me laughing all the time. He literally did whatever he could to keep a smile on my face. We went out on dates multiple times throughout the week. If we didn't have a date, I would cook to make sure we ate together at my apartment. He took care of me after a long day of work. And one of the best changes he made was the fact that he wanted to take pictures with me all the time now. I didn't have to beg him.

During this time, it was the summer and I had just bought a brand-new car. I was working an internship and two jobs alongside that to keep up with my new car payments. I was also awarded a scholarship to live in the campus apartments for the summer during my internship, which led to me keeping that same apartment for my last semester in the fall. Dude ended up coming to stay with me at that apartment as well. I didn't have a problem with it because we were a couple. Our original plan was to rent an actual apartment off campus together, but Dude basically had multiple reasons for why we couldn't. Nevertheless, I got over it and went with the flow. I wasn't into the arguing stuff like before, and I was enjoying our peaceful and loving relationship so much that I would rather not pick fights over things I felt I couldn't change.

The one time I did get very upset with him was when we were in my car leaving the liquor store and he had his driver's license out of his wallet. I picked it up and looked at it to make fun of his old photo when I realized the year on the card read something that wasn't adding up with his current age. Then I remembered the conversation from earlier that year with the young lady I met with. I became furious. I instantly started questioning his reasons for lying to me. He denied it again saying that his ID was a fake he used back in the day for the club and liquor store runs. Trust me, this was not the dumbest lie he ever told, but it was close to it. I was just so deep in love that I couldn't grasp the fact I was believing anything that came out of his mouth without question. We stopped talking for a few days.

The day we met for him to apologize and "make it right," he had his mama on the phone. She was willing to cover for him about his age, but one of his sisters stepped in and confirmed his actual date of birth to us all. That's how I found out he was 27 years old and would be 28 in just a couple months. At the time I was only 21 and didn't care about the age difference because I liked older men anyway. I was just upset at the fact that he lied to me about it. I was upset that someone told me about this situation months ago and I didn't believe her because I was desperate to have him as my man.

However, I didn't stay upset. I first remembered that I was in love with him. Then his mama talked to me personally and assured me that if I loved him for real, this was a situation worth working out. That's what I did. I worked it out. Dude eventually came clean about everything else as well. He mentioned that he wasn't in school, he didn't currently have a job outside of party promoting, and he also didn't have anywhere to live outside of staying with me and other friends' places he would crash at. Not to mention he no longer had a car either due to what I had done. I had already decided that I was going to forgive and stay in the relationship to be with him. So I was willing to work it all out after he came clean.

Since Dude didn't have anything to hide anymore, he became his true authentic self. I believe he knew that I was in love with him, and I was willing to work with whatever he brought to the table. We took a few road trips, and I went home with him and met his family. It was such an amazing experience. I saw how family oriented he was. I saw how much his family loved and adored him while he was home. We had such an amazing time, and I knew for a fact I was getting to know the real him. We also took a road trip to my people back in Detroit, which only lasted two days because I was just going home to renew my license. I knew for a fact that a few of my family members were not into Dude at all, but I didn't let that hinder my love for him.

After family visits and extended road trips, we began talking about marriage, kids, and what life would be like after I graduated. I already knew I was headed to L.A. after graduation, so I started working on plans for us together. I would come up with different things he could get into while I worked on my hosting career. I started looking for jobs he could apply to in advance. I was really making my dream our dream. And he was down with it for the most part. He saw how hard I worked, and I believe that made him a little relaxed.

He started feeling so relaxed that I felt like he may have been a little lazy. My work ethic was exceeding his during this time. Although I "side-eyed" the situation, I never really unpacked it fully. I would wake up at 6 AM every morning to go to my internship. Then I would come home around 11 AM and go to my first job as a server at a restaurant. While getting ready for that job, I would notice Dude was now up watching *Family Guy*. That work shift would end around 3 or 4 PM, and I would grab food from there and take it home to him. Dude would still be watching *Family Guy*. I would change clothes and go to my second job waitressing until around 11 PM. After work, I would grab food for us and bring it home. Dude would still be sitting on our bed watching *Family Guy*. Whenever I didn't bring food from a job, I would come home and cook for us. This was the routine for at least 4 out of 5 weekdays. Instead of feeling irritated with him about how my weekdays went, I started hating *Family Guy*.

On the weekends we were still going out together and he was still getting super drunk. His drunken nights would oftentimes cause arguments if I wasn't as drunk as he was to put up with absolutely anything. I was willing to overlook the fact that I was basically taking care of the both of us because he paid for all our dates. He even filled up the gas tank of my car every time he used it. Whenever I didn't feel like going to the club with him, he would take my car and still go do what he had to do for the parties, so in my eyes, he was still working. We were still loving on each other daily. We would have nights where we just rode around in my car laughing and talking about everything. He would perform his own R&B concerts for me in my bedroom and that was the cutest thing ever to me.

My love for him and the things we did together kept our relationship tight. It was tight enough to ignore all the bull-crap and keep trying to be better. It wasn't until I started taking my relationship with God seriously that things started to get a little rocky. He would always come to church with me whenever I asked him. In my whole college life, I hadn't missed a Sunday of church unless I was out of town or just too hung over to make it, which was rare. I went to church with hangovers most Sundays as well. I was raised going to church every Sunday, and I wasn't allowing too many "turnt" nights to stop me. As time led up for me to graduate, I started to attend weekly Bible studies as well. Dude had never been to the weekly Bible studies and didn't want to go at first. When he finally came with me, I was excited. He wouldn't come every week like I did, but he tried his best to get with the program.

During this time, I started attempting to fast and pray. My fasts would always end sooner than planned because I would have sex with Dude whenever he wanted it. If it happened during a fast, I would quit because I knew that was wrong. My whole situation was wrong, but I was still learning and growing. I taught him how to pray, and we prayed together as much as we could. We would call in to the weekly prayer calls together and have post Bible Study discussions together as well.

Although I was growing in God tremendously, I wanted him to come up with me and as quickly as I was moving. I didn't want to mature in faith without him. I thought of a great idea one day and asked him to join a fast with me. I thought with him being on this fast with me, we wouldn't break it due to sex. That was the one thing I told him was off limits along with the foods we were giving up. However, he couldn't hold out, and if he couldn't then I couldn't.

As time went by, I started to feel conviction about my relationship with Dude as I continued to pursue God wholeheartedly. I ignored everything that started coming up about what was wrong with us. Our romantic endeavors were still in place, and our love was only growing stronger in my eyes. I began bringing up the topic of abstaining from sex until we got married, because I started to feel a real tug on my heart in that area. We had already talked about moving to L.A. together and eventually marrying.

He told me that he was a grown man and that my sex was something I couldn't take from him. I never brought it up again after that. One night, I came home from Bible study and he was about to go out. I don't know how the conversation started, but Dude began explaining to me how he didn't want the things I wanted in a relationship with God. He said, "You want to fast and do all this other stuff, and I don't want that. You probably want to speak in tongues when you pray, and I don't want that neither." He said a few other things, as well, but that part struck me so hard because I was literally just praying in tongues on my drive home.

I was so sad at this realization that I didn't argue with him or say anything back. I just let him take my car and go that night. I began thinking of how to plan my next fast to seek God about this relationship. I wasn't going to pray and asked if he was "the one" because I just knew this was possible for me. I just wanted God to change his heart and mindset on so many things. I wanted him to be more like me. I was deeply invested in what we had. I loved his family, and he loved mine. We had fun together all the time. We had many spontaneous dates. We were the life of the party together in most instances. He made me laugh, cry, smile, and feel good all at the same time. I had already planned our life together after graduation. We had been through so much and our love outweighed it all. I just knew he was my person.

A few days after that conversation, I was at work and Dude basically broke up with me through a text. I could not believe it. I left work early that day. I went home, dressed up as cute as I could, then pulled up on him at the club where he was working. I interrupted him at the door and took him to the patio of the club to talk to him. I had so many questions as to why he was doing this to me. Nothing came of his mouth but lies. He was drunk as well. So I knew he wasn't capable of the truth right then and there.

I waited until later that night when he said he was coming to pick up his things. Then, I seduced him and begged him to stay after. When we woke up the next morning, he resumed packing his things and leaving. I was so confused. I thought our nightcap would fix whatever was wrong with us like it always did. But it didn't.

We got into a major fight that morning because he lost my car keys before heading out. That fight lasted for a few weeks and in the process, I lost my job for not showing up. I also wasn't able to go buy new keys until he finally agreed to help me out. I found myself getting drunk multiple nights crying my eyes out about our break-up. I just could not believe he had broken up with me. It literally crushed me to my core.

I had a couple months of school left when we broke up, but I didn't stop having sex with him until I graduated. Although we were no longer a couple, he came over for a nightcap whenever I asked. In return, whenever he wanted me, I let him come over as well. I did somehow think our nightcaps would bring us back together eventually, but they didn't. Things went back to the way they started. He would leave my apartment like nothing happened each time, and it always broke my heart because I actually still wanted to be with him. I felt like I had lost my best friend, because that is what he had become to me over time. I was still in denial that the relationship had ended.

How This Worked For Me

"You shall have no other gods before Me."

Exodus 20:3 (NKJV)

It is very clear that I had made this man an idol in my life. Anything you put before God is an idol. I basically worshipped this man in a sense. And when my worship wasn't enough, he went back to being his true authentic self, the one that he hid from me under the conniving and deceitful tactics he used to lure me in. All of my efforts to create a beautiful relationship from a jacked-up foundation had crumbled. That is what happens when you know to pray before entering relationships, but you don't. I had a clue that I should have sought God, but I was still very immature in my faith and constantly giving in to all of my fleshly desires.

I had a few other distractions happening in that time of my life, but I pushed through them all to focus on him. He was my outlet when I was vulnerable and grieving. He was the person I called when I needed to talk. Before I prayed about anything, I took it to him first. I was a mess when I was with him. I was often drunk every night with this man. After a while, I noticed the toxicity in his alcoholic behavior, so it slowed my drinking down a bit. One of us had to be sober some of the time. Even in my sobriety, I ignored all the red flags of the disaster that was ahead of me.

This man would spend all this time giving me attention, and I loved it. I didn't realize this time and attention was due to Dude not having anything else going on with himself. I began to plan my life out with someone who had no drive, no ambition, and no goals in life outside of finding girls to take care of him. I believe he broke up with me that night because he knew I was slowly but surely waking up from the lust spell I was under.

Dude and I were unequally yoked in so many ways. I had a passion for my gifts, and he didn't. I had dreams for my career, and he had dreams while he slept all day. I was walking blindly into a toxic relationship and trying to create a marriage out of it eventually. It never would have worked out because my heart really started changing as I was making an effort to grow closer to God. When I started praying about the relationship, the conviction I was feeling was telling me to leave him alone, but I couldn't. I didn't want to. We were yoked together at the soul.

I had connected myself to him through sex and that kind of connection created strongholds. Yes, soul ties are real. The worst part was that when I left for L.A., I called to check on him, and he already started sleeping with another girl. Someone he told me he didn't like months prior when I heard rumors. He told me that he was a man and he had his needs. He said I shouldn't be upset because I had left. This was after we had talks of him flying out to visit me. At that point it was time to break that soul tie. It wasn't easy, but God helped me through it as I grew in a relationship with Him. A few months later, I was baptized at church and I literally felt the freedom from all chains of soul ties and strongholds on that day. I was able to start my sexual abstinence journey that I have been on ever since.

God saved me from physical and mental heartache that I could have expected down the road. He couldn't possibly have placed me with a man who had no physical self-control when that was what I was striving for. Never think that you need someone. If you feel it in your spirit to let someone go, trust that. Have courage. It doesn't matter how long you've been friends, or how long you've been in a relationship with them. You have to realize that in this life everybody can't go with you. If God wants your crowd and your load to be lighter, let Him bring you up! You can't be in unequally yoked relationships and think they're going to prosper. They make your load heavier than what it has to be. Don't let anyone sink your ship. When it is time to end a relationship, end it. End it for you. End it for them.

Chapter Eight

Repossession Works

When I first bought my car, it was one of the most incredible things to ever happen to me. I was in summer school at TSU, going into my senior semester. I had just started interning at NewsChannel 5+. I was nervous about how I was going to make it to my internship every day and to work without a car. I had been managing without a car my whole college life because I always had friends with cars. But it was the summertime, and everyone had gone home or worked jobs and couldn't rearrange their schedules for me. I started using Uber, but the expenses for that amounted to what I imagined a week's worth of gas would cost. I didn't know what I was going to do, but I trusted God that something was going to happen regarding my transportation issue. My Aunty Kesha had just bought a new car at a dealership back home. She knew I was in need of a car, so she told me to come home to Detroit and go to that same dealership and buy a car. I just knew that was my miracle waiting for me. It came out of nowhere, so it could only be God.

That next day, I hopped on the greyhound bus and went home. When I arrived, my Aunty Meechie picked me up from the bus station and took me right to the dealership. Aunty Kesha and the car salesmen were waiting for me when I arrived. I filled out some paperwork for the dealership, and then they took me outside to choose my car before they even let me know if I was approved to buy a car that day or not. As soon as I saw Ruby (what I later named the car), I knew she was mine. She was a brand new 2015 Red Chrysler 200. No one had ever driven her off that lot before, not even for a test drive. She was in a line up with some other cars, and I walked straight past the other cars to reach her. I took her for a test drive, and I fell into a deeper love for her than the love at first sight feeling I already had. When I returned to the dealership, they told me I would have to put $1,000 down at the least in order to drive her off the lot. I didn't have any money at all. All I had was my credit card that I brought to use for the gas money it would take to drive my car back to Nashville. I just had faith that I was leaving with that car.

I went into the bathroom of the dealership, I kneeled down on the floor, and then I prayed to God about making a way for me to leave with that car. I knew my credit was brand new and all I had so far with it was my student credit card. The only way I would be able to leave that lot with my car was if a miracle from Him took place. When I stood up from praying, I shouted, praised and thanked God in advance for my car. I went outside and I had Aunty Kesha take pictures of me with the car. The guys at the dealership called me into their office to fill out more paperwork. They left the office for about ten minutes, then the next thing I know; they were bringing me contracts to sign for them to release the car to me. It was literally a miracle. The very one I had just finished praying for.

I went outside to that lot, and I could not even touch my car without thanking Jesus for being so miraculous. As I walked closer to the car, my feet got lighter like I was walking on clouds.

Everything began to go in slow motion for me. I sat in my car and before I could even drive, I asked Aunty Meechie to get in and pray with me. The moment I was in was so surreal. I was about to drive off that lot with my very first car, that just so happened to be a brand new 2015 vehicle in the year 2015. What an amazing blessing. (Especially for a young woman who grew up in poverty.) Then to top it all off, I was leaving that place with no money down. I walked on that lot with no money in my pockets, and by the grace of God, still left that same lot with a brand-new car.

I named my car Gorgeous Ruby Woo Carter. I took the name Ruby Woo from the red Mac lipstick that my car reminded me of when I first saw her. I asked everyone to call her Ruby for short. Ruby meant everything in the world to me. I drove her back to Nashville with so much joy and gratitude. I literally talked to Ruby every day like a pet or something. I took the best care of her that I could. I loved my car with everything in me. When I graduated in December, I packed everything I owned from my campus apartment into my car, and then I began my journey to chasing my dreams. The fact that everything I owned was able to fit inside of my car was like a confirming sign that I needed to go straight to L.A.

I remember Taraji P. Henson coming to TSU earlier that spring for one of our Distinguished Lecture Series. After her speech at the series, she did a smaller and private master class for the mass communications students. I was in the front row with my journal out taking all the notes I could. She talked about the life journey of pursuing a career in entertainment. Her main point that she drove home to us was "Be Your Own Boss!" She wanted us to write our own stuff, create our own projects, and not let anyone take our creativity from us. There was one thing she said that struck me and opened my eyes to what was possible. She mentioned that she knew some of us would want to move to L.A. like she did. I was one of those people. She told us that when we made it to L.A., the first thing we will most likely hear is No! But don't let that stop you. She said, "All you need to make it in L.A. is a car and a dream!" So when I packed every piece of my entire life into Ruby the day after I graduated, I knew that message was specifically for me! I had My Car and I most definitely had My Dream!

I left Nashville and drove to Atlanta first. Although I planned to stay there for a while, my dream was to relocate to Los Angeles. It took me almost two months to tap into my faith to just get up and go. When I finally decided to take that drive across the country from Atlanta to L.A., Ruby was there. She had my back. She was down to ride for me. When it was time for me to go, Ruby was kicking up that dirt with no complaints. At that time, it was early 2016 when gas prices were at the lowest they had been in years, so it only took $18 to fill her up. I was grateful that she was good on gas, and the most I had to pay for regarding my journey with her was an oil change. I paid my car note up to last me while I searched for a job there.

On the road it was just me, Jesus, and my car. I drove from Atlanta all the way to L.A. with Ruby. I had Tina Campbell's solo album, *It's Personal*, on repeat the whole way there. That album helped me make it here. That's the album that played a huge part in turning my car into my *War Room*. If you haven't seen the movie *War Room* yet, then let me explain what that term means to me. A War Room is a place where you go to reverence God; to spend time with God. It's a place where you go into prayer like you're on a battlefield fighting for your life against the enemy and negative spirits that try to attack the very essence of your existence. It's the place where you literally feel God's presence like He's face to face with you, hugging you, holding you, and letting you know that He hears every single petition you're making out to Him in that very moment. In that place you find your peace in the center of chaos. You find your hope in the midst of discouragement. And the best part is you find your praise right in the middle of a trial. That place for me was my car.

For the first four months of my life in L.A., I experienced some things that made me run to my car to pray to God. I cried my eyes out in my car when things were rough, and believe me when I say, things got rough often. No matter where I was going, I prayed every single time I put my car in drive. Jesus was my favorite and most frequent passenger. Traffic in L.A. is extremely horrible, but I enjoyed the long drives because I used those times to have intimate conversations with God that strengthened my life and helped my spirit mature in Him. Sometimes I would even turn off all music and talk to God in the silence and stillness I was able to create in my car. My car wasn't the only place I used for prayer, praise, and worship, but it was the only place I had to call my own.

I didn't have a home to call my own. I was working little jobs here and there, but nothing was steady. I couldn't afford an apartment at the time. Those two months of car note payments had already been up and I was now on the extended past due list. I figured that something was going to come through for me, and the money received would be enough to catch me up. With the whole L.A. life transition not going the way I hoped for, I wasn't giving up. I kept telling myself that I was okay, because I had a car and a dream. And for a while I really believed that it was all I had.

On the last Tuesday evening in June 2016, I was in a real bad space. I was having one of the worst moments of my life, so I thought. I was confused about everything. I didn't know what

God wanted me to do. I didn't know where God wanted me to go. I was sitting on the bedroom floor of my friend's apartment, crying my eyes out. I was crying because I hate the feeling of not knowing. I hate feeling like I am putting my best foot forward and receiving nothing in return. I felt like I should have had it all together by now. I had been in L.A. for four whole months, and I still had yet to find a stable job. I still didn't have my own place to live. I had tried everything I thought I could possibly do in my own power. I had just worked for the BET Awards the week prior, and I still had yet to believe that I was blessed. Mainly because my blessings didn't look like what I thought they should have. As I was crying, I decided to write an entry in my Spiritual Journal, telling God how I was feeling. This is what I wrote,

> *"Dear God,*
>
> *I feel like I really am trying. And if I'm not, please show me how I can try harder. If you want me to write, how come you don't give me the ideas to write? Why isn't my creativity kicking in when I sit down to write? What am I supposed to do? I don't like not knowing and being clueless. I really want to have some type of idea of what I'm supposed to be doing in my life. How come I don't feel like you're guiding me if you are? How come you haven't sent a mentor to help me? I prayed for one; a good one. I need help! God I can't do this by myself! And if you won't physically tell me what to do or help, then I need somebody to do it. I need direction. I need guidance! I need HELP!! I need a job or some steady income. I can't shoot my show without money. I need a team, but the team has to be paid too.*
>
> *God I don't get it. I know all things work together, but what am I supposed to do when it doesn't feel like it? How can you allow*

me to feel stuck? Why of all days is my computer not working? Why don't I feel like I'm learning anything in this season of my life? What's wrong with me? Why can't I be great? Why is it so easy for me to get discouraged? Why do I have to be the one with the hard story? Why me?"

After writing this I immediately started to cry again because every time I talked to God it sounded the same. My thoughts, emotions and feelings were all over the place. I picked up my phone, turned the camera app on, and then pressed record. I felt the need to record a video trying to encourage myself. In my video I was honest about how I was feeling. My goal was to motivate myself through the video as if I was talking to someone else who wasn't me, but was going through a similar situation. I was looking at myself in the camera, and to me, I looked so weak, distraught, and broken down. The weakness I saw on my face was something I never wanted to see again. So I quoted a scripture to myself to help me pull it together. I played the song "Rise Up" by Andra Day, and that song really resonated in my spirit as I was singing it. It made me want to actually rise up. It made me want to give myself hope, so I did. And I pulled on every ounce of strength that I had left in my body, and I stood up off that floor. I decided to accept everything I was doing wrong in the situation and I made up in my mind to get myself together.

I dressed, styled my hair and prepared to go to ASCEND!, which is a Bible study that DeVon Franklin hosts in L.A. every last Tuesday of the month. I thought to myself that if I could just go to church to hear a word from God, it would be the icing on the cake to my newfound hope that I was currently experiencing. One of the people I was staying with wanted to tag along so she got ready with me. Every time this particular friend and

I would go somewhere together, she usually drove. This time I told her that I would drive, since I was already planning to go by myself. We were both in expectation to go receive a blessing. As we walked outside towards where I was parked, I couldn't see my car. I had just gained so much hope, joy, and strength that I couldn't think negatively. However, I was walking towards something that clearly wasn't there.

We arrived at the spot where I was parked, and there was black car there instead of my red one that I had left there. So my friend looked at me and asked, "Why are we right here? Where's Ruby?" And I answered, "Ruby is not where I left her." She asked me if I was sure that I had parked there, and I told her that I would have never walked to that spot if I wasn't sure. It was my favorite parking spot. It was in the shade, under a tree, and I loved parking there for that exact reason. I had moved my car to that spot earlier that morning to avoid a street sweeping ticket on the other side of the street. I recall sitting there in that shade praying and reading my Bible before I went back in to start my day. I looked at that car in front of me for about two minutes before I said anything else. There was no possible reason for my car to have been towed. Instantly I resorted to what was the only explanation left. I knew my car had been repossessed. And at that moment, every ounce of newfound hope and strength I had just gained, left me.

The repossession of my car struck my faith like nothing I have ever felt before. It was an extremely hard thing for me to experience. I was so shaken up by the loss, that I almost forgot where my faith was. It took a toll on me for a long time. I honestly believe I went through all of the stages of grief with this thing. I know this happens to people in the world, but I wasn't prepared for it to happen to me. I was a couple months behind on my car payments, but I just knew God was going to help me take care of it. I spent time trying to make money just to survive in L.A., so my car payments fell by the wayside in the midst. I was couch hopping with no real place to call home, but I always had my car to run to when there was nowhere else to go.

Of course, I tried what I could to get my car back, but when I didn't get it back, I fell into such a weak disposition that took me so many months to break out of. I didn't understand how I could pray so hard for something, believe with my whole heart, have unmovable faith about my car note being taken care of, and then it was repossessed. I didn't understand it. The hurt and anger I expressed was ultimately directed toward God, because I thought He didn't care enough to help me. I thought He wasn't listening to my petitions and my requests. I thought my faith alone was supposed to be enough to sustain me. This pain I felt turned into blaming myself for moving to L.A. I blamed myself for not being more prepared. I blamed myself for all of the things that I could have done. I felt like life was turning for the worst and having faith in the process was too hard.

How This Worked For Me

"Consider it pure joy, my brothers and sisters, whenever you face trials of many kinds, because you know that the testing of your faith produces perseverance. Let perseverance finish its work so that you may be mature and complete, not lacking anything."

James 1:1-4 (NIV)

Losing my very beloved car became a struggle. The struggle turned into a trial that lasted in months of sorrow for me. I understood the truth of me no longer being able to afford my car, but that truth didn't stop it from hurting me so deeply. I didn't know how I would come back from that honestly. I cried about it a lot. I was already struggling so badly in my attempt to start my career, and this discouraged me even more. I felt like God was putting me through a test like Job from the Bible. But I didn't want that kind of test. I felt like I already had nothing, so why would He allow the only thing I did have to be taken from me?

God never gives you a test that doesn't teach you something and ultimately bless you in the end. Since my car was my "war room," I felt like I didn't have a private place to pray anymore. I told God my lack of prayers during that time was because they took my secret place from me. Eventually I pulled myself together and had to shake off the sadness concerning it. I had to be able to create a place for me and God to dwell anywhere. I started going on walks and runs around the neighborhoods I was living in to pray. I prayed in bathrooms of wherever I stayed and where I worked. I made sure God knew that although the place I loved to spend time with Him in was gone, I wouldn't stop praying.

My car was gone, but that didn't stop me from wanting to chase my dreams. I had to use public transportation to keep pushing towards my destiny. I couldn't stay stuck there. It produced the type of patience in me that I never thought possible. I was able to endure the bus and weird smelling train stations. I was able to learn how to maneuver through this huge city with tons of great people maneuvering with me. When the enemy thought I would crumble, I endured. When he thought I would mope, I rejoiced and thanked God. When he thought I would give up on God, I allowed God to take my spirit and mold it into what He considers maturity. I endured the test because I knew that it would bless me.

Once I finally got a steady income, I was able to create a Lyft and Uber budget that didn't exceed the things I needed every month. It actually worked out well. If there were events that I was attending with friends, I always had a ride. God blessed me with friends out here who didn't mind picking me up and taking me wherever we were going together. He also blessed me with people who checked on me for grocery store runs and errands I may have needed to take care of. I was able to cultivate some of the most Divine Relationships I've ever encountered by needing a ride! Car rides with friends have been so filled with revelation, worship, therapeutic conversations, confirmation receiving, healing, comedy, and absolute fun. I have built so many great relationships with people in their cars.

Once everything came around full circle, and I finally had a place of my own and secured a blessing of a job, I was able to walk to that job every day because it was only a 10 minute walk distance from my new home. I didn't even need a car to function in my everyday life after that happened. What was perfected inside of me became greater than what happened to me. When a test comes, get excited, because there is something in it that God has for you. By the end of the test, you have a sense of wholeness that gives you confirmation to know that with God, you are complete, needing nothing. Once you get to that point, you realize how much the test was worth it.

Chapter Nine

Rejection Works

I hate being rejected. I really do. The feelings that usually follow rejection make it all worse. I feel disappointed, hurt, frustrated, and weary all in one. After that it sometimes leads to anxiety, anger, and resentment. It's almost as if I can't fathom the thought of not being wanted or accepted. I sometimes question my identity, or even forget who I am depending how hard it hit me. I would always think that I was the problem, or something was absolutely wrong with me in the instances of facing rejection. Rejection sometimes creates stress and worry to the point where I couldn't possibly think that it is a good thing. However, my dealings with rejection have always led me on a different path than the way I attended to go. If I have ever faced consistent rejection in my life it has definitely been during my L.A. journey.

This journey all started when I graduated college. I had no idea how prepared you had to be for this kind of life transition until it arrived. The after-college life is nothing to play with. Even if you never went to college, I'm sure you can understand that the real world outside of school is not a safe zone. When you are in school, you are basically playing it safe in life. I mean, tuition does cost money, so you are hustling to stay in school and take care of yourself, but when school is no longer a place of protection from the outside world, you're in trouble. Now it is up to you to make sure that you have your own place, utilities, food, transportation, your own everything, and none of that is included in your tuition anymore. There are people who rent their own apartments and things of that nature while they're in school, but for someone like me, who had no help and couldn't afford that lifestyle, leaving my college apartment was pretty scary.

The day after I graduated, I cried my eyes out because I wasn't sure where my life was headed. I knew that I had been speaking my whole college life about how I was moving to L.A. after graduation, and although I tried my best to make the connection prior to graduation, I still wasn't prepared when it arrived. I had options of different places I could go, and different things I could do, but none of them were what I truly wanted. I could have gone back home to Detroit and worked with my aunty. I could've moved to Kentucky with my best friend Stephanie and made a life there while I prepared for California. I could have actually stayed in Atlanta where I had my daddy to help me out until I got my life together. The options were there, but the desire to take those options into consideration felt like I would lose everything I had worked for.

I felt like I worked really hard during this journey of chasing my dreams by starting out with an education. I tried my best to follow the blueprint Oprah Winfrey laid out for me. I attended TSU because she did. I got involved in radio there because that's how she got started. I interned at NewsChannel 5 where she was once the anchor. I even perfected my craft in school by having my own self-titled talk show. I worked really hard and I excelled in all of my mass communication classes. I just knew the preparation from everything I did to gain experience in this field would work out for me. Not only that, the bishop of my church in college, Bishop Joseph Walker, III, did a whole Bible study series on faith during my last few weeks of school. Every time I attended Bible study, it was like he was speaking directly to me. I literally kept receiving confirmation after confirmation to just take that leap of faith and move to L.A. to chase my dreams. I had the knowledge, the experience, and the faith.

I went to visit Stephanie in Kentucky for a week. I received a lot of encouragement from her. She did let me know that I could spend time there to prepare, but I was still eager to go straight to L.A. When she left to go home to Detroit for the holidays, I couldn't tag along. I felt as though if I went back to Detroit, I would be stuck there for a while. I knew that the state I was in was fragile and going home where the majority of my family was would make me comfortable in that moment. It was easy for me. So I went to Atlanta. I was advised to go there, stay with daddy and family, save up for about 6 months, then finally go to L.A. when I was more prepared. The only problem with the plan was that it wasn't mine, or God's plan. The idea had been suggested to me by people who cared about my well-being and wanted me to play it safe. I appreciated the advice and absolutely took it initially.

Everything in me was dying day by day while I was in Atlanta. Before graduating I had so much fire built up in me that I was ready to hit the road to L.A. and never look back. I was telling people that I believed my faith would take me there and keep me there. When I realized what I was saying sounded so terrifying to actually accomplish, I didn't do it at first. I let fear and the advice of others keep me from doing what I believed God could do. That was an error in my faith. I cried nearly every day during that time. I had diagnosed myself with post-graduation depression. The weight of me not being where I desired to be was heavy.

Staying with my daddy didn't last long either after having a family discussion where I finally expressed to my stepmom how she made me feel as a kid. It was too much.

I ended up going to stay with one of my federated sisters in my NACWC organization. Tangeia really took care of me. She made sure I was comfortable and didn't add pressure to the post-graduation anxiety I was feeling. I only stayed there a few weeks before my big decision to move. During my time there I applied to so many jobs and went on so many interviews. The crazy thing is that in every interview I had, I was discussing my dreams with them, and they would literally encourage me to step out on faith. Since the jobs had nothing to do with what I wanted, I found myself going into these conversations talking about what I wanted. Sometimes talking about my dreams came out like word-vomit. I realized my "Dream Talk" wasn't going to take me anywhere, so during the last interview I went on, I was reserved and ready to learn what I needed to do to make some money. I ended up getting a call back from them offering me that job, but by the time that happened I had already made a decision to go.

I was watching a sermon by Priscilla Shirer that put the icing on the cake for me. In this sermon she talked about Gideon in the book of Judges where he received so many confirmations from God that He would get the victory. In addition to that, God made him decrease the number of soldiers he had to 300 against 3 other armies of thousands. She put an emphasis on that part and told us that it was okay if we felt like we didn't have enough to work with. The victory we received would be to the glory of God so that no one would be able to say they did it, but God! God did it for me! I was thinking I didn't have enough money saved up, but I received so many confirmations that I needed to go. My faith was telling me that God would make a way no matter how much

I had, because He would get the glory from this. Then I thought to myself, "Why would I try to land jobs and build a life here for a short period of time, just to have to start over again when I go to L.A.?" I made the decision that I would trust God. I knew He was the one telling me to go. All the confirmations added up. It was time for me to make up in my mind that I would push past my fear and to the leap of faith. So I did.

I loaded in my car, took the $400 I had in my account and hit the road! I told my daddy what I was going to do and he hooked me up with a long distance cousin in Orange County. I had somewhere to land when I got there instantly after making the decision. On the way there I stopped in Texas to visit my uncle for a few days. He was very encouraging in my decision. After that, I stopped in Arizona to visit my Aunty Tara and family for about a week. To my amusement, they encouraged me on the journey as well after trying to convince me to live there instead. My Aunty Tara made sure she prayed over me and sent me with food on my way out the door. Overall it took about two weeks from the time I left Atlanta to finally arrive in Los Angeles, California.

Lord knows I was so full of joy when I first exited off the highway and found myself in downtown L.A. I literally worshipped and praised God as soon as I saw the welcome sign. I felt a sense of peace just sweep over me. DTLA didn't look like what I expected it to, but I wasn't discouraged by that at all. Everything in me felt like I had made the right decision. I was grateful for the air. I was grateful for the people walking around. I was even grateful for all of the construction I saw going on. I made a couple trips around in a circle trying to get out of downtown, but I loved it. I took in the experience of arriving in L.A. for only a day, then I instantly hit the ground running.

I came up with a plan to start looking for jobs in tv show production. My main goal was talk shows, but I found myself applying to everything tv related. The entry level position for this field is Production Assistant (PA). I was on *staffmeup.com*, *entertainmentcareers.net*, and a few other entertainment industry recruitment sites looking for PA jobs. For some reason I was under the impression that hosting jobs were going to be too hard to find. I applied and auditioned for a few within my first year here, but then my search for them came to a halt. I told myself I could continue hosting my own things on my YouTube channel, but for work I should be focusing on the production side. I thought that if I started at an entry level PA position on talk shows, then someone would discover my talents and eventually let me produce my own show. I don't know where I came up with this "brilliant" idea, but I'm assuming now that it was a result of fear. I thought I came out here ready to roll, but some parts of me were hesitant.

A few days after my arrival in L.A., I was contacted to interview for the OWN Network! This was a PA job for a very famous therapeutic reality show. I studied all night for this particular interview. I reached out to people to gain insight about what I should say and how I should go about answering questions. I prayed to God all night and early that morning about allowing me to have the job. I believed this job opportunity would be a sign from God that I made the right decision in moving to L.A. All of the details added up. I attempted to follow Oprah's journey to the best of my ability. I felt confirmation that it was time for me to go to L.A. a few weeks prior. Although Tyra Banks was my initial inspiration for my chosen career, Oprah Winfrey was the best to ever do it, and if I could just land this job with her network then this would be the start of my dreams coming true! I just knew this was my job. I met all of the qualifications, I had the entry level experience needed, and I thought my interview was absolutely outstanding! They started talking to me and making plans about our upcoming season together during the interview.

I waited by my computer for my congratulations email all night long. Nothing came. Then the next day I woke up excited and waiting. Finally, I saw an email notification, and I was ready to celebrate when I read it, but it said they were going with another candidate. I could not believe it. I just knew this job was mine. They even gave me the impression that I was a great fit for the job while interviewing with them. That was the very first rejection letter that ever made me cry. However, it wouldn't be the last. I went on so many interviews almost every other day from that point on, and all of them ended with rejection emails. I had yet to know what the word "congratulations" looked like anymore. I was rejected from every single job I applied for in the industry for a full 18 months.

Facing rejection after rejection led me to believe I had made the wrong decision in moving to L.A. In the meantime, I had worked a few jobs like Dunkin Donuts for a week and a check cashing place for a couple months. I did a few background gigs, got a production job for the BET Awards in 2016, and even started acting. Most of the production jobs I was able to do were volunteer for passion projects. With all the rejection I faced, I was feeling really discouraged. I forgot who I was. I went dark and low to depression at some point. I questioned if my faith move was just a "me" move. I questioned if I was good enough. I questioned if I should just move back home to Detroit multiple times.

It wasn't until I had a meeting with someone from a talent agency that told me to stop applying to work in television production. She said my hosting gift would make room for me. She told me that all I needed to do was get myself in front of the camera as much as possible and watch it work out for me. The crazy thing is, I had wasted so much time here looking for those jobs that I almost forgot the reason I had come to this "City of Dreams." When she said that, I snapped back into myself and hit the ground running with everything she said. So many people had approved my crazy plan to work in production. A lot of the connections I had made out here told me they would help me to find jobs in that area and never did. It wasn't until I met with this talent agent who I was introduced to through a friend, that everything clicked for me. My journey out here had finally been put into perspective. It wasn't until that moment that I was able to shake off all of the feelings of being rejected for so long had brought me.

How This Worked For Me

"Coming to Him as to a living stone, rejected indeed by men, but chosen by God and precious, you also, as living stones, are being built up a spiritual house, a holy priesthood, to offer up spiritual sacrifices acceptable to God through Jesus Christ."

1 Peter 2:4-5 (NKJV)

The rejection I faced for a whole year and some change happened because those jobs weren't even for me! God had another plan for the route I was supposed to take because He cared for me. I am precious to Him. We all are. He doesn't want His children to be disheartened, depressed, or downcast when people reject us. I had to go back and unpack the possible reasons for rejection when I finally snapped out of hopelessness. For the jobs I was applying, I was fully prepared and capable to perform in excellence. It wasn't that I didn't fit the profile for what they were looking for. It wasn't that I was a bad person either. Those opportunities just simply were not mine! They belonged to someone else.

In the midst of me being jobless I did so many other things to account for the time spent in my development along the way. I took background gigs, paid audience work, and I was an on-call temp for different entertainment companies. While I did that, I was able to work on my acting gift which landed me roles in two short films and a web series. I booked a gig acting as a defendant for a court show one time, and my grandma saw me on TV! That was definitely a highlight for me. I also worked on passion projects with friends as much as I could during that time. Then I finally produced a talk show entitled *Kingdom Talk* during a really hard time in my journey here. *Kingdom Talk* was near and dear to my heart because it created an environment for like minded individuals to have open conversations about the struggles we have as faith-filled millennials in our community. That was my very own first self-produced passion project that I was able to see all the way through to the finish while still finding my way in L.A.

Once I was finally blessed with a job, it wasn't in production like I was shooting for all that time. It was a receptionist position for the office of the Television Academy—the office of the *Emmys*. This job blessed me in so many ways, and is still a blessing even as I type this out. I have a front row opportunity to learn the ins and outs of the television industry while I work. I went from receptionist, to HR Administrator, then promoted to HR Coordinator in only my first two years working with this company. I didn't know why God had me learning and growing in the realm of Human Resources at first, but I now have a few ideas of what I will be doing with these skills next. He literally placed me at this job for a reason and I see the fruits of it every chance I get.

Since my job is on the nine to five, Monday through Friday kind of schedule, I still had the flexibility to work on my hosting gift after work and on the weekends. I was hosting after-shows for After Buzz TV Networks live on YouTube every week. I was literally there at least two nights and sometimes three nights a week after work. Black Hollywood Live is an affiliated network, and I hosted a show on there as well. I really grew a fan base with some of my favorite shows, and had the opportunity to interview a few of my favorite stars on those shows. This gave me the ability to keep myself on camera as much as possible as I had been advised to do.

I started auditioning for hosting jobs and I wasn't getting call backs most of the time. Then somehow, every amazing opportunity I received found me instead. I was able to do some of my best work through having friends who believed in my giftedness. I hosted a live showcase on a biweekly schedule for a few months for one of my favorite couples here. I was also blessed with an opportunity to host a show with friends on the radio. We hosted the millennial segment of Dr. J's Uncensored on 102.3 KJLH. Although that only lasted a season, it was one of my favorite opportunities with hosting.

I remember sitting in a shared Lyft ride home one night, and the driver and second passenger were discussing a topic they had just heard on the radio. I noticed the conversation when I climbed in the car, and I asked them what station they were listening to. Before the other passenger could answer, he recognized my voice, and said, "That was you! We were just listening to you!" That was such a beautiful moment for me, and we expounded on the topic the whole way home. Moments like that gave me assurance that I was on the right path.

Rejection didn't stop me. I was applying to the wrong jobs anyway. When I started going out for things I was supposed to, opportunities started happening for me. I mentioned that I didn't get some of the hosting gigs I went out for recently, but I also turned some down. One of them was for a prominent entertainment news company too. I really believe in the phrase "what God has for me is for me." He has been ordering my steps since I was able to walk. Now that I desire to talk for a living, I trust Him to orchestrate where that takes me too. I thank God for every closed door, and I believe in my heart He has some open ones on my horizon.

Chapter Ten

Fire Works

I had been homeless in L.A. for a year and 9 months before renting my apartment. I had all of my things packed in my car for the first 6 months before the repossession situation and lost everything. During all of this I was couch hopping at people's apartments. Some of those couches I rented, and some only let me stay for a short amount of time with little contribution. I will create another outlet to go into detail about my "Couch Tour." However, this chapter is the glory reign of when I was finally able to rent my own apartment.

In 2017, a few weeks after starting my job, I was ready to find my own place. I was looking for a one-bedroom apartment because I just knew that I didn't want any roommates. After searching high and low for an affordable one-bedroom in my area, I realized they were way out of my budget for the current salary I was making. One day when I was walking out of an apartment tour in discouragement of the costs, I ran into an old friend that I had lived with before. We stayed together on another friend's futon back in 2016. Come to find out she was apartment searching as well. I knew that if I was going to have to live with anyone, it may as well be someone I already knew. The good thing about already knowing her was that we also had lived together before, so it was a no brainer because she knew how I lived. We decided to be roommates and from then on it was go time.

I started circling the block and surrounding neighborhoods on foot to find a place. I mostly went during my lunch breaks at work because I needed to find something that was in the area of where I worked. I stumbled across this one building and dialed the number. The leasing manager picked up and said they had availability for a two-bedroom after some people were moving out at the end of the month. We scheduled the tour for then. When we finally toured the place, we liked the set up, but the space was small. It also looked familiar as I had been to an apartment just like it while visiting my great friend Lami. This was in a different building than Lami's place because hers was on another block.

I remember Lami's place having the exact same set up, but it looked bigger in size because they had a balcony outside their living room door. So, I asked the leasing manager if this apartment was supposed to have a balcony. She told me that the company who owned the building actually owned 3 buildings in the area that are the same. She said she had another opening coming up in the building around the corner. I told her that I had friends who lived in that building. When I told her the names, she told me the available apartment was opening up right next doors to theirs! I said, "We'll take it."

I was so excited to be living next door to Lami! She is literally my best friend I have in L.A., my prayer partner, sister in Christ, roll dog, comedian, adventure buddy, homegirl, human journal, shoulder to cry on, and so much more. Friendship with her has been a blessing, and to be in arms reach of her was going to be amazing for me. What was also amazing was that this new apartment had everything my roommate and I wanted. It had all of the amenities except a washer and dryer in the unit. But since those were on site, we were okay with it. My main desire was to have a bathroom that was not inside of my room. The apartment was dual master apartments, meaning both rooms in the apartment were the "master bedroom" and had their own bathroom. The issue was that in every other apartment both bathrooms were inside each of the rooms. I knew I would have a lot of guests in my place, so I didn't want people having to travel through my room to get to my bathroom. Turns out, the apartment we chose had a room with my exact desires. Both the room and the bathroom were huge and separated by a mini hallway. The icing on the cake was that this place was in both of our budgets.

The day I moved into my place, I was blessed with so much furniture and essential needs! I was blessed with a beautiful all white bed set, coffee table, bar stools, plates, cups, cooking wear, silverware, refrigerator, dining room set, and couch and chair set. I was even given a TV. I literally didn't have to buy anything but toiletries, cleaning supplies, and the décor for all the things I received. I was living in overflow! God had exceeded my expectations of allowing me to finally be on my own two feet. Although I was splitting rent costs from having a roommate, I was still able to provide for myself and carry my own weight with bills and sometimes hers too. I was finally gaining a sense of stability in my life and I loved it. I was excited for the journey ahead.

My roommate and I decorated the apartment in such a way that it felt like a home. It was very comfortable and beautiful. I loved being there. I had so many functions and events at my place. I cooked a lot of times for myself and others whenever I wanted. I was so close to my job that I came home for lunch almost all of the time. I had friends over frequently. A few family members even came to visit at some point. I created a space there of love and celebration for anything. My roommate stayed in her room or wasn't home the majority of the time, so it was almost as if I had the place to myself. She came out to enjoy festivities with friends of mine that she knew whenever she felt comfortable. I was at peace with our living partnership and had no complaints! My apartment was my pride and joy. I had so much fun in my place. I loved every minute of it. I said to myself that I wasn't leaving that place until I was ready to get me a penthouse downtown or getting married.

In late November of 2019, two days before Thanksgiving, my apartment caught on fire. It happened in my bathroom while I was in there. I was sitting down in a chair that I brought in my bathroom to finish my passion twists in the mirror. It was 1:30 AM, and I only stayed up that late to do them so I wouldn't go to work the next day with my hair looking crazy. Next thing I knew, the vent above the shower exploded and went up into flames. I ducked from the explosion and then panicked before reaching for my phone to dial 911. I literally couldn't find my phone that was right in front of me because of what I was experiencing. It took me a second to snap back into reality and I grabbed my phone and ran out of there. Before I could open the door, I saw liquid fire begin to pour down from the ceiling of the bathroom into the tub as smoke filled the room. Instantly my heart dropped, adrenaline started rushing, and I feared for my life.

After dialing 911, I banged on my roommate's door to wake her up, and we ran out of the apartment. She ran down the stairs and I ran next door to bang on Lami's door to wake her up. I ran outside to avoid the possibilities of getting caught in the fire and called her a few times. After about 5 minutes I saw her coming out of the building as the fire department pulled up. There was no building manager or property manager on site when this happened. I called the emergency line for someone to come out, and no one ever showed up on our behalf from the apartment. I spoke to the maintenance contractor that night and he couldn't come until later that morning.

We stayed outside from approximately 1:30 AM until 4:00 AM. We went back up in between that because they said it was safe to go in and grab a few things. However, as soon as we went up they came back and put us out because the fire traveled upward to the bathroom above mine on the second floor. This time the fire alarm finally went off in the building and sent everyone else who lived there out in their pajamas like the rest of us. I waited outside praying that the fire didn't transfer to my room. Since my room was facing the front of the building, I saw when the firemen had to kick the window screens out in order to let the smoke out.

When we returned to our apartment it was only to grab a few overnight things, because the place was filled with smoke and ashes from the fire in the bathroom. My room was actually untouched thank God. Beside all the ash footprints and things from the bathroom that they threw in there, it was completely fine. The only thing destroyed was the bathroom and majority of things in it. We could not stay there because it was completely unlivable for the time being. Our electricity in the whole apartment was shut off by LAFD because the cause of the fire was electrical wiring failure in the pipes of the building.

That night my life flashed before my eyes. It was a very traumatic experience for me. Had I not been in the bathroom that night I may not have noticed the fire in time. If I was in the shower, I would have burned to death. If I had been sleeping, my whole apartment could have burned. And I could have lost everything, including my life. I was struggling mentally with this whole fire situation, and I could not believe God would allow me to go through such a thing. The worst part of all of this was my apartment company did absolutely nothing for me. They didn't even have anywhere to put me while my apartment was being worked on. I still had to pay full rent although I had to go 3 weeks without a bathroom. I even had to clean up all the ashes and sweep and mop my entire apartment once I returned to it. The insurance I had through the company only took care of damages that I made to the apartment and not my personal belongings I lost. Although the fire was the building's fault, the apartment company filed a claim with the insurance for the damages as if it was my fault.

During that time, I had to use Lami's bathroom and shower because my roommate made me feel uncomfortable using her half of our apartment. I spent a lot of time at Lami's and she helped me through my disappointment with God. It was a very hard and frustrating time for me. I kept praying that He would fix my apartment company so they would meet the demands I made, and they didn't. I even attempted taking the legal route concerning it, but a good lawyer wasn't in my budget. I was so hurt and discouraged through this entire circumstance because I really did love my apartment. I didn't want to have to leave, but these people had me messed up and I couldn't go out like that.

I decided I was going to leave the apartment because of how the company handled the situation. I asked my roommate to tag along because I thought I needed a roommate. She said no, she was fine with the apartment because her side had been untouched and unbothered. She was good where she was. I knew finding an affordable one-bedroom place would be a challenge, but I had to put on my big girl panties and get to work. During the process I felt a little scared, and I questioned if I should even leave my apartment. I thought I was maybe just upset because of the fire and how the apartment company handled it. Plus, I had an extremely brand-new bathroom that I saw being built with my own eyes. I thought I could stay and chill, and just move on with my life like none of this ever happened. Once I started thinking like that, God started sending me dreams. These dreams were warning dreams that it was time for me to move out of there. Not only did that scare me even more, but it put a fire under me to do as if the actual fire wasn't enough.

How This Worked For Me

"When you pass through the waters, I will be with you; and when you pass through the rivers, they will not sweep over you. When you walk through the fire, you will not be burned; the flames will not set you ablaze."

Isaiah 43:2 (NIV)

First and foremost, I am grateful to have made it out of a fire alive and unharmed! That is not everyone's story. I was going through a traumatic situation and God still protected my life! I realize the grace of God in my life through this whole situation. He knew something like this would happen, and it motivated me to do the very thing He wanted me to do which was MOVE! I needed to move to fully prepare for the transition He has me in now. There were old friends, a roommate, and bad habits that were attached to that place. I loved my place so much, but He had to move me out of my comfort zone so that I could do what He has called me to do.

God did indeed bless me to be able to have a one-bedroom apartment that was affordable and discounted just for me. It was still in the same area; however, I could no longer walk to work. I only caught a Lyft to my job for a week, then the next thing I knew, we were under quarantine due to the pandemic, and I was on work from home orders. God gave me my own place, then shut the world down while I was left alone with Him. At first, I was really going through it. I couldn't stand not seeing my people because I love being around people. I wanted to still chill and hang with friends, watch TV, and movies and talk about life all day. Then I started losing friendships. It was a little bizarre. I went from going through a fire to what was beginning to feel like an emotional storm. I didn't understand what was happening in the world and why everything was changing so fast. I was heartbroken by everything instantly.

I felt the Holy Spirit leading me to pick up my computer and complete this book, but I just could not at the time. I started writing this book in 2016 and ever since then, I would write a chapter once or twice throughout the year and put it back down. I also knew that God was calling me to a time of consecration for prayer, fasting, and repentance. I had drifted so far from spending daily time with God for a while. I thought it was the fire that made me fall off, but the fire was literally the call to come back. He wanted to prune and refine me during this time.

Before moving into my new apartment, I went through a period where I was smoking weed and drinking pretty often to cope with my living transition. I was staying on my friends' couch for a few weeks before I got my stuff together for my new place. I was distraught that I had found myself in a situation like this yet again in L.A. Since the fire wasn't my fault, I blamed God. I felt like He didn't fight against the apartment company for me like I prayed for Him to. I wanted to see revenge on my behalf because they had pissed me off so much. I tried to replace His presence with the substances I was using to cope with. By the time I moved into my own apartment, the conviction I was feeling every time I indulged was so heavy that I had to just stop smoking and drinking all together. There's no peace in the things we use to cope. The peace we need is only found in the presence of God. You can't replace the presence of God with substances.

During this quarantine I started having moments when something from my past, be it recent or childhood, would just pop up in my brain out of nowhere and make me super emotional. The thoughts were so uncomfortable that I would immediately look on Instagram and redirect my focus to whatever I saw on there. I would dive deep into other people's timelines, stories, and what-ever parts of their lives they shared with the world. Then if that didn't work, I would look up a comedian and watch funny videos on Instagram to laugh hard and loud enough to drown out the sorrow that was swelling up in the back of my throat.

When I got tired of scrolling for hours on Instagram, I started binge watching *Living Single* from the first season, and I laughed the whole time. Every time I heard myself laugh, it shocked me. It made me think to myself, "I was about to sit here and cry for what? For nothing! Especially not when there's so much to laugh at out here." The sound of my laughter masked every pain I was originally feeling. Whenever I would stop laughing, a strange and painful feeling of anxiety would pierce my heart and sit there until I laughed again. It was a lot. Way too much for me. The worst part was I was living in a place alone for the first time ever, and it was hard mentally.

The anxiety led me to watch inspirational videos on YouTube. I would sit and listen to people who shared what they had been receiving from the Lord in their quiet times with God. Since dis-traction was weighing heavy and it was hard for me to have my own quiet time, other people's devotion became quite interesting to me. Those videos were the only things that could calm my mind. Then somehow every word of wisdom or divine revelation started to sound the same. They were all saying, "Spend time in the presence of God; be obedient to what He's telling you to do in His presence; and lastly, write your book." Pretty weird right? Because how did they know what God was telling me to do?

I finally decided that I would get in God's presence. After wise counsel from one of the people whose videos I watched, and a friend holding me accountable through a very convicting text message, I finally went on a fast. It was during a 21 day liquid fast that God delivered me from so much. I can't even begin to explain the healing and transformations that took place in my heart. Most importantly, He gave me a strong desire to live in a constant state of repentance. And in my repentance, He delivered me from being a lukewarm Christian. He literally gave me an "I don't want to" for all the things I used to do that were not of Him. For that, I will forever be grateful.

Instead of masking all of the cries that were coming up from things of my past, I had to let it all out. The kind of cries that came out of me during that fast were brutal. However, crying out to God about it all gave me strength to be obedient in picking this book back up to finally complete it. I originally wanted to write this book just to tell my testimonies of what the Lord has done for me. But then, it turned into something deeper. It created a space of healing for me. The telling of the testimonies, covered in the blood of Jesus has healed, and is continuing to heal me from all trauma, mistakes, confusions, failures, and total misunderstandings that seemed to have had me bound.

If it took that fire for me to get to a place by myself when the quarantine hit, then that fire did exactly what it was supposed to do. Although that fire didn't consume me physically, God had set another fire in me that consumed my heart and refined me to get all the things He wanted out. I am still a work in progress for the Lord, and I will always be. We don't get to a place in our lives where we arrive. In Him we go from glory to glory. During those transitions we will experience tests and trials. Nothing that happens in our lives is by accident or random. God knew it would happen. He okayed it. Then He perfectly and strategically orchestrated whatever it would be to work together for us.

Conclusion

The Called

"And we know that all things work together for good to those who love God, to those who are the called according to His Purpose."

Romans 8:28 (NKJV)

We broke down the beginning of this scripture in the *Introduction.* The last part of this scripture states that this promise applies to all of those *who love God, to those who are the called according to His purpose.* How do you know that you love God? In John 14:15 (NLT) Jesus tells people, "If you love me, obey my commands." If you do what God tells you to do, if you move when God tells you to move, if you are open to what God thinks about the decisions you make, before you make them, then you know that you love God. Spending time with God in prayer, worship, and reading His word are also expressions of love to Him.

Putting your trust in God when everything around you looks like it's crumbling is one of the most powerful expressions of love for God that we can have. Sometimes we allow our mistakes and bad decisions to pull us away from God because we don't feel worthy enough of partaking in what He has for us. But self-condemnation is a tool the enemy uses to distract you from God's grace and unfailing love. God loves you, and He knows that you love Him, so why would He try to destroy you?

The attacks on your life are not from God, and they are meant to take you down. But God has a way of taking what was supposed to tear you down and building wings with it so that you can fly over it and whatever else there is to come. You are *called* for a reason, and it is *according to His purpose* that He helps you to make it through. Once you have fully accepted the call, you let God know that you're willing to ride this thing out with Him. God's purpose and plan for your life has amazing heights and depths that you would have never even dream of experiencing. In order to get there, you have to grow. The things in your life that are happening to you even now are meant to help you in that growth. Nothing happens to you "just because." You're only growing stronger and stronger as you continue to live. And the best part of living is the fact that no matter what, everything will be all good.

What does it mean to be called? To have a deep yearning for the things of God and desiring to have a heart like Christ. It's a longing to want to do the things God placed inside of you to do in an attempt to bring God glory. It's having a heart to love and serve God's people because we want to please Him. It is what you feel when you know there is more to you than what life has already presented you thus far, but you believe that "more" comes from the direction of God. Once you realize that you are called, you have to answer the phone for that call every single day. The call will take work.

Answering the call requires healing, deliverance, heart mending, and becoming whole. Though things tried to take you out in life, to send you on different paths, the fact that it didn't means

God wanted to cause that thing to work for your good. While working for your good, it helps you in achieving everything else you need to do within your call. It's not ideal for a doctor to be cut up and bleeding while trying to perform surgery on a patient in desperate need. It's not ideal for the leader of an Alcoholics Anonymous meeting to be drunk while trying to help the members at the gathering. The only way to help heal others in areas of your personal expertise, is to have already overcome yourself.

Look into your own life. Think about the things God has called you to do. Are there any areas of your heart that may still be bleeding pertaining to your call? Have you faced any issues, rejections, traumas, heartbreaks, or pain that could possibly prevent you from operating in the fullness of that call? If so, that's okay. It's why I wrote this book. I'm right there with you, encouraging you to seek God about the areas of your life that hurt the most. Sit down and ask the questions you've always wanted to know pertaining to why something "had to happen" in your life. Write it all out if you need to.

Allow God to show you how whatever it is worked for your good. The healing process will take time. It will probably be hard work as well. However, God promises that if we are strong and courageous, He will be with us wherever we go. Trust Him. So when the process is finished, you can thank God for the very thing that the enemy tried to use to destroy you. Nothing he throws at you will ever keep you bound or stagnant. It is all working together for you. So I want you to be free! Be free in your heart, mind, soul, body and spirit. Then you can walk out your calling with confidence in Him. And now you know, that's good.

About The Author

Porchia Carter is an author, talk show host, actress, and producer. She has talents in many of the arts and has decided to use her gifts and talents to serve God's people in any capacity. She refers to herself as the Purpose Driven Creative. Her mission in life is to inspire young people to live their dreams while trusting God through the process of seeing those dreams manifest.

Porchia was born and raised in Detroit, Michigan for the majority of her life. She currently lives in Los Angeles, California where she has used her gifts of dance in ministry. She has hosted for various online networks and radio shows. And she has used her acting gifts to star in a short film and web-series. Some of her very own productions include shows like *The Porchia Carter Show*, *Kingdom Talk*, and *Men Do Talk*.

Porchia has a very charismatic personality and can be a bit goofy and animated sometimes. Her vivacious persona does not take away from the fact that she is a faith-filled believer of Jesus Christ. She is a walking ministry attempting to make disciples in order to fulfill the great commission. Her passion and love for God is what helps her put her best foot forward in all that she does. Her greatest desire is for all to see the light within her and be directed towards Christ.